THE MISSING GENERATION

A PRACTICAL GUIDE TO 20S - 30S MINISTRY

KAY MUMFORD

The Missing Generation
Kay Mumford and 10Publishing © 2012.

Published by 10Publishing, a division of 10ofThose Limited.
ISBN 978-1-906173-92-0

Design and Typeset by: Mike Thorpe / Design Chapel
Printed in the UK by CPI Group (UK) Ltd, Croydon, CR0 4YY

10Publishing, a division of 10ofthose.com
9D Centurion Court, Farrington, Leyland, PR25 3UQ, England.
Email: info@10ofthose.com
Website: www.10ofthose.com

Some of the names in this book have been changed for anonymity.

Dedication

THIS BOOK IS DEDICATED TO THE LATE REVD MARK ASHTON,
MY FORMER BOSS, PASTOR AND FRIEND,
WHO TAUGHT AND MODELLED THE CHRISTIAN LIFE TO ME,
AND TO THE CONGREGATION OF ST ANDREW
THE GREAT CHURCH, CAMBRIDGE,
WHO HAVE DEMONSTRATED COMMITMENT TO TRUTH,
A LOVING COMMUNITY,
A PASSION FOR THE LOST, AND SACRIFICIAL SERVICE.

Contents

Acknowledgements

THANKS TO THE STAFF AND WARDENS OF ST ANDREW THE GREAT
FOR PROVIDING ME WITH TIME TO WRITE THIS BOOK,
TO ROSEMARY DAWSON AND SHEILA JACOBS
FOR THEIR HELP WITH EDITING
AND TO THE MANY PEOPLE WHO HAVE WRITTEN CONTRIBUTIONS.

SPECIAL THANKS TO MY HUSBAND, ALAN,
FOR ALL HIS ENCOURAGEMENT AND SUPPORT IN
WRITING THIS BOOK.

Introduction

It's Sunday morning. You sip your coffee and start to browse through a Christian magazine. One article catches your attention – it's called 'The Missing Generation'. It claims that the average lifespan of a church is approximately forty years. You grab the magazine and head off to church.

The first song gets underway, and you take the opportunity to look around. Over on the left are a handful of children, which is encouraging, but you are concerned about the future leadership of the group. The current leader needs to step down; they have run out of ideas and energy. You fear that the lack of enthusiastic young leaders will mean the children eventually stop coming.

Then you spot the small group of teenagers clustered together in the corner, looking into the distance, distracted by thoughts of exams and university applications. You've seen it before – they head off to uni and don't come back.

The next age group you see are the forties to fifties, mostly parents: tired, overcommitted, concerned about their children's behaviour and latest school reports. The rest of the congregation are retired – core members who are always there; faithful and loyal, prayerful for the church.

The song draws to a close, and you realize that there is a group of people conspicuous by their absence. The twenties and thirties age group are missing – no young singles, no young professionals. The main focus of this book will be on singles and those married without children. (Once people are married with children, they are covered by the children's and families' ministry of the church.) These are the people who could have been running the children's work, the future home-group leaders, the next generation of the church. The missing generation.

You resolve to show the article to your church leadership after the service. It's an area of concern, and something has to be done. If not, your church will become just another statistic.

This book is written for local churches to explore the reasons for investing in ministry to those in their twenties and thirties. It looks at practical and simple steps that you can take as a church to attract this age group. It will suggest a vision for fruitful ministry among them, and how we as churches can make this vision a reality.

I write as someone who is passionate about ministry to this age group and who has experience of working with them. My hope is that this book will help to produce disciples of Jesus among those in their twenties and thirties, and secure the future generation of your church. This goal is really achievable if we pray, catch the vision and invest in these young adults. The consequences of ignoring them will be seen in the years to come with dying, ageing and empty churches.

> THE CONSEQUENCES OF IGNORING THE MISSING GENERATION WILL BE SEEN IN THE YEARS TO COME WITH DYING, AGEING AND EMPTY CHURCHES.

CHAPTER 1

Mind the Gap

Missing generation

If your church is missing the twenties to thirties age group, you are not alone. Sadly, this is the common story across the UK.

Research by The Evangelical Alliance[1] found that the number of people between 20 and 29 attending church had declined by 62 per cent in the last twenty-five years, compared to a total drop of 37 per cent across all age groups. They concluded that there was a crisis in the church in the UK. Since the 1980s, people in their twenties are the least frequent churchgoers. We are missing a whole generation of people.

Maybe you are in a large fellowship, and haven't noticed that there is a missing generation across our nation's churches. The larger the church, the greater the proportion of those attending that will be under 30. Within London, 57 per cent of churchgoers in their twenties attend churches – leaving smaller ones outside London with a shortage.[2]

Why are they missing?

Unimpressed

Sometimes there has been a bad experience with a church leader. Sometimes the hurtful act is specific, such as a youth leader being too critical or overbearing. For some it's rhetorical, either from the pulpit, in a small-group study, or over a meal. For others it has been physical, taking the form of sexual or other forms of abuse. But many claim a wound they can trace back to church that has never healed.

Why? In part, because the church rarely seeks forgiveness.

Under-resourced
Churches can struggle to find enthusiastic, committed and able leaders to work with their existing children and teenagers. The children become more interested in Sunday activities outside church, and there are not the key personal relationships with leaders to keep them attending.

University
Even if we have managed to keep our teenagers in church life, we often lose them when they leave home for university. It may be a time of growth for them as Christians, but there is an increasing trend of finding a job away from home once their course has finished.

EVEN IF WE HAVE MANAGED TO KEEP OUR TEENAGERS IN CHURCH LIFE, WE OFTEN LOSE THEM WHEN THEY LEAVE HOME FOR UNIVERSITY.

Others who were less rooted may have drifted from faith altogether at university. Maybe it was a relationship with an unbeliever, the attraction of the party lifestyle, freedom from restrictions, or an unhealthy focus on academic achievement. It may have been lecturers or fellow students questioning their beliefs, causing doubts. All these things can all lead to spiritual drift and lack of Christian commitment.

Non-Christians

A whole generation has either walked away from Christianity, dismissing it as irrelevant, or have been so completely unaware of its message that they haven't even considered it.

For the last seven years, I have been leading discussion groups with non-Christians in their twenties and thirties. In the twenty-one groups of people who were asked about their beliefs and world-views, these were consistently held by all.

- **There is no truth. There is no God who defines what truth is.**
- **All world-views and beliefs are equal. We must respect and accept all views.**
- **People who promote exclusive truth are intolerant and offensive.**
- **There isn't one moral code that fits all – each person has the freedom to decide for themselves what is right.**
- **The ultimate goal in life is happiness. If you have found something that makes you happy, that is all you need.**
- **The Bible is irrelevant and old-fashioned; we live in a different world with modern values. It has no authority for today.**

With such beliefs as these, the average 20-something is not going to come to church unless these deeply held assumptions are dramatically challenged. For the non-Christians I have met, this challenge happened when they met Christians (often at work) who were distinctive and leading a consistent, attractive, God-centred life.

What are the consequences of ignoring the missing generation?

Dying churches

If the lifespan of a local church is only forty years, then without the twenties to thirties we will gradually see dying congregations.

We need twenties to thirties to marry, have children and provide the next generation of churchgoers. Pure survival is the main reason for thinking about this issue. For the most part, evangelism to those in their twenties and thirties will be more effectively done by their peer group.

The people most effective in reaching this generation are Christians in that age range. UCCF (the Christian Union movement) is one of a number of groups that exist to reach out to undergraduate students (18 to 21), but this leaves the church with the responsibility of reaching out to those doing postgraduate courses in university, young professionals and workers.

Future church leaders

Without a group of twenties and thirties, our churches

struggle to provide the next generation of home-group leaders, leadership teams, and children's workers. The ministry of a church will grow in size and effectiveness when there are leaders with the time and energy to drive it forward. A large proportion of people in their twenties are either single or without children, so may have more spare time to devote to church activities in the evenings and on Sundays.

Financial resources

Without a group of young workers, our churches will struggle to grow financially. Therefore they will not be generous in giving, financing church activities and evangelistic initiatives. Twenties and thirties may have more expendable income if they don't yet have the financial burden of mortgages or children. In the church I attend, this age group provides a significant proportion of our annual income from the congregation. They are the most generous givers because they can often afford to be.

> TWENTIES AND THIRTIES MAY HAVE MORE EXPENDABLE INCOME IF THEY DON'T YET HAVE THE FINANCIAL BURDEN OF MORTGAGES OR CHILDREN.

Conclusion

These three reasons alone should be enough to stir us to prayer and to action.

This missing generation is a serious problem – one that will have devastating effects of the future growth on the church.

Even if we have a core group of twenties and thirties, there are many non-Christians still to reach. We need to equip those that we have to live Jesus-centred lives, so that their distinctiveness will be attractive to a generation that is lost and searching for truth.

I hope that this book will help churches think through how they can attract Christians in their twenties and thirties, how to reach out to non-Christians in that age group, and how to nurture them so that they become fruitful disciples of Jesus.

NOTES

1. Evangelical Alliance Council document, *The 18–30 Mission: The Missing Generation?* (2009). http://www.eauk.org/church/resources/theological-articles/upload/Report-The-Missing-Generations.pdf.

2. Special English Church Census Edition, November 2006. www.ccsr.ac.uk/research/churchcensus.htm.

CHAPTER 2

Big Vision

We might be blessed to have 20s and 30s in our church, but do we have a big enough vision of what God can do through them and in them?

I conducted a survey among 400 Christians in this age group across the country, and was saddened that many said they had more than a hundred young adults in their church, but no (or very little) programme for them.

Without input and direction, groups of this age can become purely a social gathering, with a reputation for spouse-hunting. This is a wasted opportunity to teach and disciple young adults.

Why should churches invest in twenties to thirties ministry?

- Ephesians 4:12,13 instructs that the aim of church leadership and the whole body is for all of us to become mature and united in our faith in Christ. The twenties and thirties need discipling, pastoral support and Bible teaching on the specific issues they are facing.

- Teaching and discipling the twenties and thirties will benefit the ministry of the church. They will be keen to serve the congregation and become the future leaders, elders, home-group leaders, children and youth work volunteers.

- By supporting them in their evangelism, we can reach the mission field of the workplace – gaining links with schools, offices, hospitals and so on.

- Many have expendable income, and could become the best financial givers in your church.

- By investing in a small core of young adults, new people will be attracted to join.

- They will extend your vision beyond the local church. They may go to work overseas or for other UK churches.

- We need to provide an attractive forum where Christian singles can meet; otherwise they will look outside the church for marriage partners.

I want to suggest that investing in ministry to this age group is arguably the most important and strategic work your church could be doing. The consequences of not doing so could be drastic.

Let's hear how one twenties to thirties' ministry has changed the lives of individuals, and how they have benefited from being invested in by their church. Elizabeth says:

> I joined Hub, the twenties to thirties' group, when I arrived at church as a postgraduate. It was a good way to make friends my age in a large church. I found the topical teaching on Sunday evenings got me thinking much more biblically about everything, and brought clarity to areas where I'd been a bit

confused, such as singleness/marriage, why we can trust the Bible, and so on. Small-group study, going through a different book of the Bible each term, helped me read it on my own and know how to apply it more. As small groups, we were also encouraged to support each other in telling our friends about Jesus. It was a great help to have good quality regular guest events, such as jazz evenings, with great food and a gospel talk, to invite non-Christian friends to. I knew that the gospel would be clearly explained, that other people could answer any of their questions, and it would also be fun; although I had always wanted to tell my uni friends about Jesus, I hadn't quite known how to go about it. These regular events were a constant reminder to pray for my non-Christian friends, and helped keep Jesus on the agenda in our conversations.

After a year, I was encouraged to serve as a leader, which I was rather nervous about as I didn't have much experience. However, it was quite an easy place to get started in, as most of the group were my age or younger. I learned a lot through the example of more experienced leaders and training sessions in how to disciple those in my care. I read the Bible one to one weekly with an older leader, which really helped me grow in confidence to do that with others.

THESE REGULAR EVENTS WERE A CONSTANT REMINDER TO PRAY FOR MY NON-CHRISTIAN FRIENDS, AND HELPED KEEP JESUS ON THE AGENDA IN OUR CONVERSATIONS.

I love meeting up with people for a good natter, but I

began to realize that what God has to say to us is far more important than anything I say. It made sense to try to talk about what the Bible says with people in whatever context I find myself in – whether with Christians or non-Christians – over coffee, or in a small group. I learned how important it is to depend on God in prayer in discipling people, because it is He who grows the seed of His Word planted in people's lives. Over time, I realized that those in my small group and the wider church are my family, and I need to be committed to them – considering their interests as well as my own, and investing deeply in individuals as others had done in me when I first arrived. I've learned that much joy comes from serving others and following the Lord's example.

A year later I was given the opportunity to serve with a few others in organizing the programme for twenties to thirties. It was great to see in action how the Bible should shape our priorities in ministry, and how we need to keep proclaiming God's Word in every context.

> I AM VERY THANKFUL TO GOD FOR USING THE TWENTIES TO THIRTIES MINISTRY AT OUR CHURCH TO EQUIP ME FOR THE GREAT PRIVILEGE OF DISCIPLING OTHERS.

I now lead an international women's ministry in church, and although I learn new things every week and still have lots of maturing to do, I am very thankful to God for using the twenties to thirties ministry at our church to equip me for the great privilege of discipling others who will go out into all the world to make the name of Jesus known.

If you are persuaded that this group of people is worth investing in, what aims should you have for that work? Without a clear aim, nothing will be achieved.

Setting goals and vision: maturity and mission

All ministry, according to Ephesians 4, is to equip God's people for service; also, it is to help Christians to grow in spiritual maturity. This only happens when the Word of God is at the centre of all we do. Paul writes, 'We proclaim him, admonishing and teaching everyone with all wisdom, so that we may present everyone perfect in Christ' (Col. 1:28).

The second aim of ministry is mission, fulfilling the Great Commission that Jesus gave His disciples: 'All authority in heaven and on earth has been given to me. Therefore go and make disciples of all nations, baptising them in the name of the Father and of the Son and of the Holy Spirit, and teaching them to obey everything I have commanded you' (Matt. 28:18–20).

In starting and building up a ministry among young adults, it might be tempting to make the goal something other than mission and maturity – increased finances, future leaders and increasing numbers. However, these things are the fruit of the work rather than its motivation and goal.

How can we help them to become mature in their faith?

- Help them to grow in their understanding of the gospel message
- Help them to seek to glorify God in their work and witness
- Help them to live out God's Word and grow in godliness
- Encourage them to read the Bible each day for themselves
- Encourage them to spend time each day in prayer
- Encourage them to serve the church with their gifts
- Provide pastoral support with the challenges they face

How can we help them to become more mission-minded?

- Help them to articulate the gospel message to others in a clear way
- Encourage them to pray for non-Christian friends, family and work colleagues
- Encourage them to be an active witness at work, and to take opportunities
- Challenge them to see if they are living a lifestyle that commends the gospel
- Convict them about the urgency of evangelism
- Present them with the challenge to go overseas with the gospel message

These goals are what should drive and steer any twenties to thirties' ministry. It should determine our programme for them, and the priorities we invest in.

Bible study groups

One way to help them grow in maturity is to provide weekly Bible study groups specifically for them. We might be familiar with the concept of a Bible study group, but what are the reasons for keeping young adults in the same group?

Positive implications
- Socially: It will help them form deep and meaningful relationships, inside and outside the group.
- Pastorally: They will feel able to share struggles with people who are likely to understand and who may have experienced similar things, thus making it easier to carry each other's burdens.
- Relevant application: The leader can apply the passage directly to the shared struggles and issues of the young adult.
- Prayer triplets and accountability are more naturally going to form with people of the same age.
- Evangelistically: The group is more likely to socialize with each other's unbelieving friends, and be able to work together.

Negative implications
- Home groups may be lacking younger people.

- **Young adults might not know any older Christians in church.**

Some churches have got round these issues by putting young adults into a twenties to thirties' Bible study when they first arrive, maybe for a limited amount of time, after which they join a home group.

Our church has a midweek meeting for young adults on the church premises. We have a meal altogether (we buy frozen foods from a caterer) which is an important opportunity to develop friendships and community. After some quick notices, there is a short talk which introduces the passage, before people split into Bible study groups (same groups each week). We close the evening with group prayer. We aim to finish by 9 p.m. so people can get home in good time. This meeting is well attended, and everyone is very committed to it.

> WE HAVE STARTED A PROGRAMME WHICH WILL GIVE THE TWENTIES TO THIRTIES FOUNDATIONAL BIBLE TRUTHS AND DOCTRINE OVER THE COURSE OF THREE YEARS.

We have started a programme which will give the twenties to thirties foundational Bible truths and doctrine over the course of three years. Once people have completed the three years, they will move to a home group.

The three-year programme looks like this:

Year 1: Mark's Gospel.

Year 2: Bible overview: Ephesians, Romans 1 – 3.

Year 3: God's Blueprint doctrine studies:
        John 14 – 17, Amos.

We are praying that this will greatly benefit and train our young adults, and help them to be firmly rooted in the gospel and equipped to teach others. Our twenties to thirties' community is very transient, so when they move on to another church, this programme will hopefully have given them a good grounding.

Making the Bible study group work

- Keep the same groups each week for developing community and relationships.
- Mixed groups attract couples as well as singles and it is how friendships develop between the sexes. Sometimes mixed groups can lead to romantic relationships. This will need wise and careful handling and advice from small-group leaders.
- Ideally, a male and female leader is needed in each group for pastoral care.
- Leaders will need some initial training, followed by some form of regular training (see Chapter 10).
- Lead clearly and in a jargon-free way so that non-Christians feel welcome.
- Community and developing relationships are very important. Consider having a meal beforehand, a social event once a term, and a potential 'away day' together.
- Encourage leaders to write their own studies as part of their training.

- Decide what to study; a balanced diet is needed. Think about reading a Gospel, an epistle, and an Old Testament book over the year. Bible books are better to study than topics, because it is better training for the leaders in handling the Bible. Group members are being shown how to study a Bible book for themselves. As a result, they are less likely to misinterpret the passage, because the context helps to know the meaning.

- Sometimes we hold a separate Bible study group for 'baby Christians' where they may go through *Back to Basics* or *Just for Starters* courses. This is a good forum for them to ask questions.

Topical teaching

In addition to group Bible study, there is also a need for topical teaching. Many issues they face will not naturally come up in a sermon. It is also a time when you can be more practical and involve group discussion.

Our group meets on Sunday evenings after church for a varied programme, including topical teaching. This meeting picks up a broader range of people – non-Christians, newcomers, fringe, and one-off visitors. People often attend this first before committing to the main midweek meeting. We try to look at issues that young adults face in the Christian life, and provide one-off sessions on them. These always include a chance for questions, discussions and prayer.

The programme should be varied in content and style to keep it interesting. It is essential to provide food at these sessions, otherwise people leave to get food elsewhere. It is important to keep the session different from just another sermon, as people are also usually tired by then.

Courses

We sometimes run a course that stretches out between four to six weeks. This has the advantage of covering subjects in more depth, building community with those attending, and delving into some other topics.

Recently we have been offering a choice of four courses, running simultaneously on Sunday nights. Each one is a differing level of intensity, so that people can pick what they can cope with. They tend to be more committed when they have chosen and signed up for a course.

> IT IS IMPORTANT TO KEEP THE SESSION DIFFERENT FROM JUST ANOTHER SERMON, AS PEOPLE ARE ALSO USUALLY TIRED BY THEN.

Each course meets in a different venue – maybe a room at church, or someone's home. Numbers vary at each course, depending on popularity and space available in the venue.

For tried and tested ideas for topics and courses, see Appendix 3.

CHAPTER 3

Culture Shock

iPad, iPod, netbook, and smartphone – just some of the gadgets that have invaded the world in recent years. Times and technology are changing so fast that it is hard to keep up. These terms may mean nothing to you, but it's important to try to understand the world and culture that our young adults are immersed in. Lots of new pressures and distractions come with these changing times, and we need to understand and know how to be supportive.

Technology might be constantly changing, but one thing that remains fairly consistent is the hopes and dreams of the young. I conducted a survey among 396 people aged between 20 and 30, asking them what their life goals were. This is what they said:

- **To be happy and fulfilled**
- **To own a nice home**
- **To be financially secure**
- **To get married**
- **To have children**
- **To have a successful career**

The difference for this generation is the likelihood of achieving some or all of these life goals. For many, these simple dreams seem unattainable – even something as simple as being happy.

The number of young adults on anti-depressants has risen dramatically in recent years, and many seem far from happy and fulfilled. The rise of house prices means that many workers simply cannot afford a mortgage. They face an endless cycle of renting and sharing with flatmates to cut costs. One woman (aged 32) shared with me the cause of her depression. In the last eight years, she has had five house-mates, all of whom had moved out to get married. But she was still there – unable to afford to buy a house, still single, desperately wanting to be married.

Today's job market is far from secure. People are often stuck in a job that they don't enjoy, but new ones are hard to come by. Some have graduated from university and are unable to find jobs that they are qualified to do. Many fear redundancy – 'last in' is often the first to leave. Many face unemployment or a constant cycle of temping jobs.

The majority of believers in this age group desire to get married, but many find there are slim pickings from the small pool of Christians they know from church. As time goes by, the temptation to marry a willing unbeliever increases. Sadly, that is all too common. It has been my experience and that of many friends that if you are a Christian woman in her thirties there are even fewer people to choose from. Statistically, people are getting married later and later, and Christians are no different. This means that the chance of childlessness in marriage is increasing. This raises an abundance of issues. The average age for getting married for the first

STATISTICALLY, PEOPLE ARE GETTING MARRIED LATER AND LATER, AND CHRISTIANS ARE NO DIFFERENT.

time in England and Wales is 31 for men and 20 for women (http://www.bbc.co.uk/relationships/couples/life_whymarry.shtml).

The idols of this generation

An 'idol' is not usually a bad thing in itself, but it becomes unhelpful for spiritual growth when it starts to replace a source of satisfaction and security that can only be found in a relationship with Jesus. The following idols are not an exhaustive list, but are things I have seen in my life and that were identified in my survey. These harmless things can be a distraction from spiritual growth and therefore become a stumbling block. These are the areas that believers need support and accountability in – as well as biblical teaching – to keep them living as distinctive disciples of Jesus. It's important for all of us to take a step back from our everyday reality and reflect on how we can be tempted to use the following things as replacements for finding our security in Jesus.

Popularity

'How many Facebook friends do you have?' is a fairly common question among young adults. Many (myself included) have over one thousand. It can make you feel popular and well connected, but the reality is that the more time you spend on Facebook the more disconnected from real friendships you become. People have less time to invest in deep and meaningful friendships in the place where they live. Sometimes Facebook is an expression of a deep desire to belong, to be significant, to be wanted and valued.

Blogs/Twitter ('How many followers do you have?') are a good way of communicating and have many uses, but sometimes this is an expression of wanting or needing to be heard, or to feel significant. And then there are smartphones. One of their uses is easier connection, with access to email and the Internet. Ironically, smartphones or mobiles in general can be the death of any conversation or social occasion. It isn't uncommon to see friends meeting up only to have their conversations disrupted by a constant stream of text beeps.

> IRONICALLY, SMARTPHONES OR MOBILES IN GENERAL CAN BE THE DEATH OF ANY CONVERSATION OR SOCIAL OCCASION.

Relationships

'If only I were married, I would be happy and content.' It is easy for singles to look at married couples in their church and covet what they don't have. They can have unrealistic dreams that marriage will solve all their problems, and bring them the fulfilment and satisfaction that they lack. Sometimes this is due to not having many deep relationships, and for having expectations that are far from reality.

Church can be very difficult for a single person, especially in their late thirties and older. Church programmes and groups are often set up with the assumption that people are married (and have children) by a certain age. This can make singles feel excluded and sidelined. They sometimes long to be part of a couple, in order to feel part of the church community.

I have counselled many young adults (men and women) whose longing to get married makes it painful to be around couples at church. If they see marriage as their ultimate goal and only source of fulfilment, they are in danger of excluding themselves from the church family altogether. Such people need much love, prayer and support from others who share their pain – but also from the wider church family.

INCREASINGLY, YOUNG ADULTS ARE TURNING TO THE INTERNET TO FIND A ROMANTIC RELATIONSHIP.

Increasingly, young adults are turning to the Internet to find a romantic relationship. We shouldn't discourage this, especially if there are limited options locally. I met my own husband through Christian Connection, which is a very respected and safe site to recommend to Christian singles. With any Christian dating site, there is a need to be wise, careful and discerning. Not everyone who calls themselves a Christian is genuine. I found it helpful to show various profiles to a trusted friend and seek a second opinion. Of course, it may be that God has blessed someone with the gift of singleness for a specific purpose. In my case, I am thankful that God chose to keep me single into my late thirties, because it gave me so many opportunities and extra time to focus on serving God and the church. There is great blessing, joy and fulfilment that can come from serving others.

Sex

Our modern culture is obsessed with sex. Young adults are bombarded with sex talk from advertising, films, chart music, office banter, TV and the Internet. Pornography is easily accessible online and is a battleground for many Christian men. Of course, this is a problem for married people too, but the single person perhaps find themselves with less accountability and more time alone. Don't assume it's just an area of temptation for men; Christian women struggle with lust too. Such things can become secret addictions, and Christians can feel ashamed to share this with people at church.

Christian couples who are dating need to be asked if they are sleeping together, or being pure in their relationships. Sometimes we are too afraid to ask the obvious questions. We mustn't underestimate how hard it is to keep raging hormones and lust under control – even if people seem mature in their faith. If they are dating, then we need to find out if that person is a mature Christian believer. If they are not, then we lovingly need to warn them that it would be extremely unwise to be in a relationship which may lead to marrying a non-Christian. If there is no intention to marry, then they should not be in a relationship at all.

In order to help Christian couples who are dating to stay physically pure, we will need to be providing accountability and support for them from an older and wiser Christian couple.

Success

Pressure to perform well in a first job or career can become an all-consuming goal. Pleasing the boss, competitiveness with colleagues, and expectation of working long hours can squeeze out time for church commitments and meaningful relationships. If you are single, work can be the place where people search for fulfilment, self-worth, value and recognition. It can seem harmless enough – but, once established, unhelpful work patterns can be hard to change later in life. It is easy to judge people by externals; we do it unconsciously when we ask what people do for a living or which university they went to.

Image

Status updates on social networking is a daily staple according to my survey, with a large proportion admitting they were on it constantly. If you are not a Facebook user, you might be wondering why one would be tempted to look at it multiple times a day. We are a generation who play out our lives on the likes of Twitter, Facebook, Flickr and Myspace, leaving us vulnerable to crippling insecurities about how we're projecting ourselves and how we're being perceived.

Sydney-based clinical psychologist Dr Cindy Nour says that social networking can feed the feeling that you are being judged or scrutinized; if you are prone to fear or negativity, if your status does not receive many 'Likes', you can feel excluded (*Grazia* magazine, May 2012). One person wrote in the survey that if her Facebook status update did not get five 'Likes' in the first hour she would delete it for fear she had embarrassed herself.

What car do I drive? What phone do I have? What labels do I wear? Where do I go on holiday? Where do I live? What job do I have? What are my hobbies? What is my marital status? All of these (and more) make up the image culture that young adults are being judged on day by day. Another huge question for this group is, 'How do you live in this world and relate to it, without getting caught up in the values and idols of this generation?'

Leisure and entertainment

Leisure and entertainment are also big deals for young adults. It is how singles spend their time away from the pressures of work. Leisure time is seen as a right, and also as a necessity for coping with life itself.

The activities seem harmless enough – surfing the web, Facebook, Twitter, watching films or DVD box-sets, watching TV reality shows or playing Xbox computer games – but the time spent on these leisure activities in any given week or month would be quite shocking if we added them up. Many are carried out alone and don't require company, which is why they are so popular with singles.

LEISURE ACTIVITIES HAVE REPLACED JESUS AS THEIR ROUTE TO CONTENTMENT AND SECURITY.

Why are these activities so consuming and addictive? For some, they are a relief from the loneliness which can sometimes be caused by singleness, or may be escapism from a stressful and all-consuming job. When a relationship comes along, the Xbox soon starts to collect dust.

These activities are not wrong in themselves and in moderation, but problems come when young adults claim they don't have time to commit or serve at church because they are too busy. Leisure time is not something they are willing to sacrifice, because it has become a means of survival for them in the pressures of life and work. Leisure activities have replaced Jesus as their route to contentment and security.

Comfort

The idol of comfort is arguably the enemy of today's church growth. We think we have the right to an easy, comfortable life because we have embraced the lies of our modern culture. Christians in earlier generations talked much more of embracing hardships, suffering and sacrifices for the sake of the gospel. We live in a 'jacuzzi Christianity' – seeking warmth and relaxation, not a giving up of all we have for the sake of following Christ.

THE IDOL OF COMFORT IS ARGUABLY THE ENEMY OF TODAY'S CHURCH GROWTH.

I see this attitude most clearly when trying to encourage young adults to consider the mission field. They find it hard to conceive a life where they would have to give up their worldly pleasures and leisure activities in order to live somewhere difficult and unfamiliar. There are always exceptions to the rule; one of our single 30-somethings has been working in the Central African Republic, where electricity and hot water are scarce. Such examples of sacrifice and commitment are sadly becoming increasingly rare.

Money

Money in itself is not an idol, but the love of money is (1 Tim. 6:10). Getting money can become the goal as a means of bringing security and the root of acquiring things that we think will bring happiness.

Young adults are often handling incomes and financial responsibilities for the first time, and need support, godly wisdom and accountability when seeking to set down lifetime habits. For many, it is the first time they will have been in a position to give financially to the church, but they may need some help and advice in how much to give. A YouGov poll conducted in 2008 found that 90 per cent of young adults were in debt by the age of 21. One in five owed more than £10,000.[1]

These are some of the common idols and goals of this age group. We need to understand these pressures and support them in their struggles to live for Jesus in today's world.

NOTE

1. From an article by Keith Walker, senior information and research officer: '20s-30s and the church: A statistical overview'. YouGov poll in 2008 for young adults's charity, Rainer.

CHAPTER 4

Connections

As churches, we need to make sure we are connecting with the twenties to thirties, and making ourselves attractive and accessible.

You may be starting off with very few in this age group, but every church has to start somewhere. The church where I work has many young adults now, but that wasn't always the case. Like most places, the work began with just a handful of people. Here is the story of its small beginnings by Cis Rose, who started the young adults' ministry with her late husband.

> When our twenties to thirties' group (called Hub) began, it was very small, but had the same aim as today – to build up and encourage young men and women in the Christian faith.
>
> We moved to a new church building in 1980, and my husband and I perceived a need for a fellowship for the handful of postgraduates. They didn't naturally fit into the other existing programmes at church.
>
> Soon the group attracted other members, and at its best numbered between twenty and thirty-five. At that time, there were some home groups meeting on different week nights to which twenties to thirties could go, so Hub provided an alternative – with visiting speakers and a variety of other activities.

From time to time we would have a guest evening with a speaker.

The evenings began with coffee and homemade biscuits and the formal part ended with prayer. We never minded how long members lingered, and it was usually in the kitchen over the washing-up that people talked about the things that really mattered to them. We also tried to have people for meals regularly.

As the group grew in size, we needed more leaders – a man and a woman. These were members who we considered had leadership potential. We met as a leadership team on a regular basis. This was a tremendous encouragement, and over the years we had a number of people working alongside us, all of whom, I believe, are now in leadership positions in churches around the country.

OVER THE YEARS WE HAD A NUMBER OF PEOPLE WORKING ALONGSIDE US, ALL OF WHOM, I BELIEVE, ARE NOW IN LEADERSHIP POSITIONS IN CHURCHES.

We ran Hub for thirteen years, until we felt that it was time for us to hand over to new overall leaders. We loved leading this work. It was a great joy, and we formed some lasting friendships. I would say that as long as you have a home, a heart for the gospel, and a desire to encourage young adults at a time of their lives when they are establishing themselves in new jobs and forming new relationships, then you have all that is needed to start a twenties and thirties group.

Getting started

Prayer

Prayer is a good place to start. Ask God to bring to your church some Christians in their twenties and thirties, who can form a core group to build on. Pray for wisdom and provision for someone to oversee the ministry.

Leadership

Identify someone in your church who could supervise the ministry. This should be someone who has time to invest and a vision for the work. It would help if they were good at relationship-building, as this will be key for growth. It could be a single person, a married couple in their thirties to fifties, or a retired person or couple. All of these would have different qualities to bring to the work. As long as they are wise, godly and mature Christians, age does not really matter. Even if you don't have any young adults yet, you will still need someone to get the work started.

Socials

Start with advertising socials – it could be Sunday lunch in someone's home, or coffee and cakes after the evening service. Advertise the weekly time and venue on a church service sheet or website.

If you are able to include at the social a ten-minute Bible thought and some prayer, this will make it easier to develop a spiritual element to the group when it grows in size. When you have a core group, ask them what they would find helpful to have talks/discussions on, and devise a programme.

A well-advertised programme will help to draw people along. Pperhaps consider handing out programme cards at the door to anyone who comes and is of the right age.

Website

It's essential to realize that most young adults moving to a new place will choose a church by investigating church websites before they arrive. If your church doesn't have a website, then it is really worth investing time and money in one – if you wish to attract young adults. You may not have someone in-house that could design a website, but you can buy ready-made website designs that can be adapted for your own needs.

A website that is colourful, attractive, with photos, and well designed will grab their attention. They may be turned off by a badly designed website that is not attractive or not easy to use. Make sure you have a clearly visible section for them, with an eye-catching programme. Make sure you also have a contact name for further enquiries.

Attracting newcomers

- **Advertise your church services in local papers and Christian newspapers and magazines. Young adults usually move to a new place in July-September and December-January. (We don't want to alienate those not in further education, but if churches want working people these are the two main times of year that people start new jobs. So, if you can't afford to advertise every week, do it at these times.)**

- **A welcome team to look out for newcomers and tell them about the relevant activities.**

- A welcome card on chairs – a section to fill out and to be sent in for further information.
- A welcome lunch or dinner a couple of times a year where you can share the vision of your church and encourage them to start serving.
- Hospitality.
- Help with finding accommodation in the area – through the website or an accommodation file. Often the first point of contact with this age group is an enquiry about accommodation, so this is potentially a useful link with a new person moving into the neighbourhood.

Venue

Find a venue to meet in. It would help with continuity if it was the same venue each week. A lounge or comfortable room would be ideal as it would help people feel relaxed. Somewhere in the location of the church would be good if people were on foot, taking the bus or using a bicycle.

Evaluate your church

To attract twenties to thirties, we need to make sure we have something to offer them.

What will they be looking for when choosing a church?

- Clear and faithful Bible teaching
- A church that will help them grow as a Christian
- Friendly and welcoming people
- A church that offers hospitality
- Small groups for Bible study and community

- **A place where they can serve and be useful**
- **A place where they could bring non-Christians to hear the gospel**
- **For some, the quality of the music will be a factor**

We need to take a good, hard and honest look at our church and try to see it from the perspective of a newcomer.

- **How welcoming is it to the newcomer? How long before someone talks to them?**
- **How will newcomers know about your church – location, service times?**
- **Do you have a website? How attractive and useful is it?**
- **What are you currently offering to young adults?**
- **Who are the key young adults you already have? How are you investing in them?**
- **How good are your church family at hospitality?**

Evangelistic events

As a church, consider running an evangelistic event that will appeal to young adults. For ideas of events, see Appendix 1. Advertise it in local papers, through your website, and produce small invitation cards that church members can give to neighbours and work colleagues.

Planning a programme

There may be pressure from some to just have a group for young adults that meets purely for a social programme. Although building community and relationships is important, there are several reasons why I think this purely social approach is unhelpful.

- They can organize their own social lives, and will do it anyway.
- What they most need is Bible teaching, accountability, pastoral care and people to pray with – even if they don't realize it or would choose it.
- Non-Christians attending the group will hear the Bible being taught.
- This will be the way they become mature in their faith.
- This is the way to develop and train future church leaders.
- Purely social groups can become inward-looking and self-centred.
- A group that is being taught the Bible will be more effective in serving the church.

Quality Christian community and relationships are always in the context of Bible study and prayer, and these will be the things most helpful towards them maturing in Christ.

Why not consider starting each meeting with serving food, which builds community? It doesn't need to be anything fancy.

Developing the work

In time, when the ministry grows, you may need a small committee to oversee the work. They will need to take responsibility for the following:

- Planning a relevant, varied and interesting programme

- Following up non-Christians, new and fringe members
- Keeping the overall leadership of the church informed of the programme
- Booking speakers
- Planning evangelistic events
- Planning social events

Weekend away

An annual weekend (or a day away) is worth considering, as it is a chance for building community/relationships and to do some extra topical teaching. We go away once a year and have a balanced programme of free time/fun, expository teaching, with a choice of seminars on various issues.

What will stop a young adult ministry from growing?

- A programme that is too heavy, repetitive, boring or irrelevant
- A purely social programme
- Not having a leader to drive/oversee the whole group
- Lack of publicity/website to attract newcomers
- Lack of evangelism/outward-looking focus
- Cliques and unfriendliness to newcomers
- Good to have an age limit; an age limit stops older single men (over 40) from coming to the group

for the purpose of finding romance with younger women. This can be very off-putting to the girls

- Lack of support from main leadership

Summary: The key ingredients

- A small team to help plan the programme
- Someone who has the vision to run/drive the programme
- A home to meet in
- Food is essential, even if frozen pizza or cake
- Publicity
- A varied programme

CHAPTER 5:

Making Disciples

Discipleship is a weird and strange thing. I remember the first time it happened to me. I was invited round for a cup of tea with an older lady at church who I didn't know very well. After a bit of chatting, she got straight to the heart of the matter. She asked, 'How are your Quiet Times going?' I almost choked on my tea in shock at the question. I had never been asked that before. The next one was even worse: 'How is your evangelism going?' It wasn't long before I was hoping this tea-drinking session would soon be over! However, I will be eternally grateful to that person because this opened my eyes to the world of discipleship. I was a young Christian and the lady wanted to encourage, challenge and urge me to live a life worthy of the gospel.

I WAS A YOUNG CHRISTIAN AND THE LADY WANTED TO ENCOURAGE, CHALLENGE AND URGE ME TO LIVE A LIFE WORTHY OF THE GOSPEL.

Years later, I ask myself those same questions regularly and enjoy asking them of others.

Last words are always significant. Before He departed this world, Jesus gathered His closest followers and gave them these instructions: 'All authority in heaven and on earth has been given to me. Therefore go and make disciples of all nations, baptising them in the name of the Father and of the Son and of the Holy Spirit, and teaching them to obey everything I have commanded you' (Matt. 28:18–20).

There are several important things for the church to draw from these verses.

Firstly, we work under the authority of Jesus, who is Lord over heaven and earth. We don't need any further permission to proclaim the gospel than this. Secondly, Christ's followers are to be disciple-makers. This is what we are about, this is our mission. It is not just an option for some Christians, but for all of us. We are not called simply to tell people the gospel, but to disciple them – nurturing them into mature followers of Jesus. Thirdly, the scope of our mission is 'all nations'. Our vision should extend beyond our church to the corners of the earth. We cannot sit back and relax until our mission is completed. Fourthly, they are to become part of God's family, His community, with a personal relationship with Father, Son and Spirit. Lastly, each generation must pass on the teaching of Christ and stress the importance of obedience, submitting to Jesus as Lord.

> **OUR VISION SHOULD EXTEND BEYOND OUR CHURCH TO THE CORNERS OF THE EARTH.**

So, we must all be in the business of disciple-making. But what exactly does it mean to be a disciple, and how do we go about making them?

What does it mean to be a disciple of Jesus?

We could go to lots of different places in the New Testament to learn about discipleship, but I want to focus on Jesus' teaching in Luke 9 – 11.

Following Jesus involves:

- **Denying yourself** – stop putting yourself on the throne and live with Jesus as Lord.
- **Taking up your cross** – being willing to give up your rights and freedom.
- **Following Christ** – His ways and His path; suffering first, followed by glory after death.

This is not easy to hear, but Jesus says that unless we are willing to lose this life and all that it can offer, we will not be able to gain eternal life. It will involve self-denial and being obedient to God (see Luke 9:23–27). We also need to be doing these things:

- **Listening to God's voice.** The disciples heard God's voice as He gave them one simple instruction: 'This is my Son . . . listen to him' (Luke 9:35). We have so many voices that shout for our attention – the media, the world, our sinful desires – but the voice we must pay attention to is God's in His Word.
- **Putting Jesus first above every other priority** – family, work, property (see Luke 9:57–62; also Luke 14:15–35). Love the Lord your God with all that you are, and love your neighbour as much as you love yourself.

Our relationship with God needs to be nurtured and growing. Our love for others is how we express our love for God (Luke 10:25–27).

- Praying faithfully for kingdom priorities, and God's will to be done (Luke 11:1–13). Prayer is a key part of being a disciple. Are our prayers kingdom-focused, seeking God's glory, or are they are selfish?

Getting to the heart of the matter

The goal of discipleship is not education; it is capturing the heart with a deeper love for Jesus and a desire for His glory. Most Christians, if they are well taught, know how to be a disciple. The battle lies with the will and motivation – this is what the Bible calls 'the heart'. Proverbs 4:23 advises us, 'Above all else, guard your heart, for it is the wellspring of life.'

We know that a battle rages between God and the idols of our heart. The question is, who is our greatest affection for? Who do we love the most – God or ourselves?

IF OUR HEARTS ARE NOT CAPTURED BY GOD AND HIS LOVE, THEN WE WILL ALSO PUT HIM SECOND IN OUR DISCIPLESHIP.

If our hearts are not captured by God and His love, then we will also put Him second in our discipleship. Only a heart captured with the grace of God can resist temptation in order to please God.

Our discipleship of others should not just be about passing on information or simply teaching biblical truth. We need to address the will, the motivation, and the affections.

John Piper helpfully says, 'Conversion is the creation of new desires, not just new duties, new delights, not just new deeds.'[1]

If the heart is where the battle rages, we know that only God can change our priorities. Therefore, we must first and foremost pray for the person we are seeking to disciple. Pray for their heart to be captured by the love the Father has lavished on His children.

What, then, is a disciple?

A disciple is a wholehearted follower of the Lord Jesus, submitting to His rule in every aspect of their lives. We all need practical help, support and prayer to do this. We need daily encouragement and accountability with our struggles. We need godly wisdom from more mature Christians to put Jesus first in practice.

But what does it look like to disciple someone? Learn from a masterclass with Paul in 1 Thessalonians 2:1–12.

Discipleship is gospel-focused (vv. 1,2)

It can be tempting to spend time sharing our own opinions about the Christian life, but growth comes from understanding and living out the gospel. Understanding the depths of God's grace will be the best thing we can pass on to others for their growth.

Our motive should be to please God (vv. 3–6)

Our motives will be mixed as we disciple others, but we need to pray for God's help.

We may need to repent of pride or the desire to be needed or respected. When we disciple others, it must be to please God and not to make clones of ourselves, for our own glory.

Discipleship is gentle and caring (v. 7)
Like a mother nursing a baby, we are called to be patient, nurturing, gentle and caring with those we seek to disciple. It is tempting to be bossy or demanding, but this will be ineffective in bringing about lasting change.

Discipleship is sharing your life (v. 8)
Paul was deeply relational. He was willing to be vulnerable and share his life, the ups and downs, with the church. He was not someone who pretended to be sorted and without struggles. He let people in, to see his life transparently – the good and the bad. The good news is that we don't have to be perfect before we can disciple others. In fact, God can use our struggles to encourage someone else in their fight against sin.

Discipleship is hard work and effort (v. 9)
People's lives are often messy and complex. It takes time to understand and know them. We will experience tears of sadness and frustration as we watch individuals decide to live for themselves and not submit to Christ. But we will also experience great joy in watching someone decide to listen to Jesus, even when it costs them everything. Then all the effort is worthwhile.

Discipleship is caught not taught (v. 10)

Notice that Paul worked hard at making his life as example for others to follow. He sought to be 'holy, righteous and blameless' among them.

Discipleship is essentially modelling the Christian life to others. Our example in prayer, evangelism, Quiet Times, priority, family life, how we spend our money, can have a deep impact on others.

Discipleship is discipline (vv. 11,12)

Paul was like a father to the young converts – 'encouraging, comforting and urging' them to live lives worthy of the kingdom of God. Sometimes this would have involved saying the hard thing and being willing to rebuke.

Discipling twenties to thirties

- **This group really appreciates the chance to meet up with older Christians, especially those at the next or later stage of life.**
- **This is a key time in their lives, when faced with all sorts of huge decisions and life changes.**
- **They may have never been discipled before, and this is an opportunity to help them grow spiritually.**
- **It will be a way of investing in leaders for the future.**

Here is a quote from Anne – she was discipled as a young Christian:

> Studying and applying the Bible together has really helped me grow spiritually. I have always felt very

comfortable asking any kind of question, and being able to discuss how to apply God's Word to our lives has been invaluable. Praying for each other during the week has been such a blessing, and has also allowed us the opportunity to be accountable to each other. It has helped me become more prayerful ... It has helped me grow in my relationship with Jesus, knowing more of Him through His Word – not only at a head level, but more importantly at a heart level. It has helped me see the great importance of telling others about the gospel, and encouraged me to do so.

> **PRAYING FOR EACH OTHER DURING THE WEEK HAS BEEN SUCH A BLESSING, AND HAS ALSO ALLOWED US THE OPPORTUNITY TO BE ACCOUNTABLE TO EACH OTHER.**

Who should we disciple?

Everyone has different situations and time available, but we could all look out for one person to take a special interest in and develop an intentional friendship.

Look for someone who is:

- **The same gender as you, to avoid confusion and unhelpful intimacy**
- **A younger Christian who you can mentor**
- **Willing to meet up and be mentored**

This may be someone in your Bible study group, someone who has recently joined the church, a new Christian, or someone on the fringe of church life.

Getting started

Once I have identified someone to disciple, I try to get to know them better by inviting them round for coffee or dinner. I explain that a good way of growing as a Christian is to meet up and study the Bible with someone each week. I ask them if they would like to consider doing that with me.

My suggestion would be once a week, or a fortnight if time is tight. Try to decide together on a fixed time and place so you don't have to keep rearranging. You might want to suggest that these meetings will last for a year; after that, the aim should be that they meet with someone else to mentor them so they don't become unduly dependent.

Discuss what you should study together. If they are a new Christian, I suggest one of the Gospels or using a course for new Christians.

If they have been a Christian for a bit longer, I would suggest Colossians, 1 Peter or 1 Thessalonians. These letters are short and cover lots of different issues that are useful for application.

The one-to-one Bible study

When they arrive, I spend some time having a drink and catching up with them. Do something that helps them relax and is relational.

I recommend forty-five minutes for a Bible study, and about fifteen minutes praying about the applications from the passage and for each other. I would allow ninety minutes for the whole session.

The advantage of a one-to-one study is that you can be

more flexible and take more time to answer questions, follow tangents and discuss application. You can also tailor application questions to their situation, as you grow in your understanding of them.

Other ways of making disciples

Maybe you haven't got time to meet up with someone each week to study the Bible. But essentially, any relationship can be a discipling one if you start to be intentional and think about things you can do together that will encourage Christian growth and maturity.

Here are some suggestions:

- **Go on a conference together.**
- **Read a Christian book at the same time and then meet to discuss it.**
- **Form a prayer triplet.**
- **Encourage them to go on a summer camp or mission team.**
- **Recommend helpful Quiet Time material. Ask how they are getting on with reading the Bible for themselves.**
- **Pray for them, and ask regularly for prayer points.**
- **Involve them in your evangelism, so that they can observe and learn from you.**
- **Invite them on a walk, or go for a coffee where you can ask questions about their discipleship.**

Christian book clubs

Tash Moore, a small-group leader, found that having a regular book club with the girls in her group formed really deep relationships.

I've found that with relationships you reap what you sow – the more I invest, the more I enjoy the relationships, and they bear more fruit.

WITH RELATIONSHIPS YOU REAP WHAT YOU SOW – THE MORE I INVEST, THE MORE I ENJOY THE RELATIONSHIPS, AND THEY BEAR MORE FRUIT.

Over the last few years I have been learning that the first and most effective way of deepening relationships is to pray. I confess my pastoral indifference and laziness, and ask for more love and more energy and more will to serve them for His sake.

Probably the single most effective means I've come across for deepening relationships has been starting a book club. We read a Christian book together, a section at a time, meeting every couple of weeks or so. This group has encouraged the girls to relate to each other . . . they know more about each other, they're more comfortable with each other, they care more about each other's lives.

The book club gives plenty of fuel for conversation, and leads people to open up in ways they find difficult in more 'personal' areas. People respond to the text/discussion in ways that help others to really get to know them – how they think, what they're struggling with, how they view the gospel and the Christian life. This book club has been such a blessing in bonding us together, taking our relationships beyond superficial politeness and formal Bible study – and therefore helping us to really encourage each other and apply the Bible to our lives . . .

NOTE

1. John Piper, *When I Don't Desire God* (Wheaton, IL: Crossway Books, 2004).

CHAPTER 6:

Effective Evangelism

Helen is starting her first job after university, working in an office, and – as far as she can tell – is the only Christian.

She is desperate to make a good impression on her boss, who has already expressed views that mark him out as an atheist. She is also trying to make friends with her new colleagues. They are making jokes about someone who is 'religious' in another department, so she decides to keep quiet about being a Christian. More than anything, she wants to be liked and accepted by her new team.

HELEN IS NOT ALONE IN FEELING ISOLATED AND TOO FRIGHTENED TO BE OPEN ABOUT HER FAITH.

Helen decides to keep her head down low when the discussion gets round to homosexuality, and is too afraid to say what she actually believes. She knows she should say something from the Bible, but is scared to. She is afraid she might get into trouble with the management. She doesn't want to offend anyone.

Helen is not alone in feeling isolated and too frightened to be open about her faith. How can we help her, and many others who feel the same?

Creating a church that looks outwards

Your group of young adults will only become outward-looking if the wider church is actively seeking to share the gospel with the outside world.

Have a clear vision for evangelism

Is evangelism at the heart of why you exist as a church? Is it stated as an aim on all your publicity, so that church members are aware of it?

For example, you could have a simple vision statement something like this: 'As a church we aim to live for Christ and to make Him known.'

Communicate this vision

This vision needs to be a corporate one, passed on and embraced by any leaders in your church – from Sunday school teachers to Bible study leaders. This is the biggest challenge, especially if they have previously been leading without evangelism as a priority. The change of priority in them will only come about with prayer and consistent, faithful teaching of God's Word.

- **Making sure our small-group leaders are being disciled themselves and invested in is the key to growth and change. It can take a while to persuade leaders of this, and get them on board with a new vision. However, the effort and investment of time in** the short term will change an entire culture for the longer term. The effort is worth it.

Model this vision

Leaders need to be encouraged to model this priority of evangelism in their own lives. This will involve boldness in speaking about Jesus at work, asking for prayer as they witness to unbelieving friends and colleagues. They will be sharing regular encouragements and challenges of seeking to witness at work. Leaders should be modelling boldness in inviting friends to evangelistic events and courses.

Churches have cultures which breed expectations and communicate values. The following things need to be thought through, in order to make your church more outward-looking.

- **Does your church have regular events for non-Christians to attend, where the gospel is clearly explained?**

- **Does your church encourage regular prayer for non-Christians?**

- **Do you have a course explaining the gospel for non-Christians?**

- **Is your church welcoming and friendly to new people?**

- **Are there elements in your church service that would make an unbeliever feel uncomfortable?**

- **Are church members challenged about their evangelism, corporately and individually?**

- **Is the Bible taught in a clear and jargon-free way that non-Christians can understand?**

- **Does the length of your services put non-Christians off coming?**

- **Does the preacher speak as if he is aware that non-Christians are present?**

- **Are things explained in the service so that an unbeliever can understand the significance of what is taking place?**

If we are thinking about the unbeliever as we plan our church services and activities, we will help them to feel welcome. More significantly, we will give Christians confidence to bring their unbelieving friends, family and colleagues to church.

Creating a culture of evangelism among young adults

Even if your church is already outward-looking, it is easy for a twenties to thirties' group to be unconcerned about evangelism. Typically, the group is only seen as a social gathering for Christians – a place to make friends, and even meet your future spouse. The temptation for these groups is to spend all their social time together, leaving little time for developing meaningful relationships with work colleagues and other non-believing friends or neighbours. Likewise, Bible study groups are naturally inward-looking, with little encouragement or accountability regarding evangelism.

From my experience, there are some things you can do to give an inward-looking group a heart for evangelism.

- **Make sure they are clear on the gospel themselves. Study Romans 1 – 5 together in small groups; have a teaching day on the gospel message. Can they explain the gospel to you?**

- **Make sure they know how to explain the gospel to others. Provide some practical training in sharing the gospel. This will take away some of the fear of evangelism that people have. Cover subjects like how to share your testimony with an unbeliever, learning a gospel outline, and by running a course in apologetics. This is a helpful way to equip Christians with biblical answers to the common objections to the gospel, and also might be something that attracts outsiders. It will also help them to be firmly rooted when they have doubts about common questions such as suffering, and the authority of the Bible.**

- Have a book for the term for everyone to read on the importance of evangelism (e.g. *Know and Tell the Gospel* by John Chapman).[1]

- Have a lending library of books that will help people in their evangelism.

- Clearly state the aim of evangelism on all your publicity.

- **Make sure they are developing friendships with non-Christians.**

- **Encourage group prayer for each other's witness to non-Christian friends, neighbours and colleagues.**

- Choose leaders who model evangelism and hold it as a priority.
- Ask them what events their unbelieving friends would come to, and develop a series of regular evangelistic events.
- Include testimonies of people who have become Christians, and how it happened. This can be inspiring and motivating.
- Interview people who are sharing their faith at work to learn from their experiences.
- Encourage them to invite an unbelieving friend to social events.
- Pray for them to have a heart to share the gospel; pray for the Spirit to give them boldness as they seek to speak out about Jesus. The battleground is our hearts and motivations.

In order to create a culture of evangelism among twenties to thirties' groups, we need to take a long-term view. Changing a culture doesn't happen overnight. The emphasis and priority of speaking the gospel will need to be consistently and persistently communicated in all the group does. Once the group's culture and emphasis has changed, it can be a powerful and effective tool for bringing non-Christians to know Jesus.

Equipping individuals in personal evangelism

Even in an age where universal truth is rejected and people are suspicious of religion, there is still enormous power in the personal testimony of the Christian believer. We could help each learn how to share their story of faith in a way that is accessible to those who don't know Christ. This will mean explaining their story in a jargon-free way and in a clear and concise manner.

We could help our young adults learn to share their story by using the following three questions:

1) **What were you like and what did you believe before becoming a Christian?**

2) **What factors brought you into a relationship with Jesus?**

3) **What has it been like for you to follow Jesus? Talk frankly about your joys and struggles.**

When I hear testimonies from young adults who have recently come to faith, it is usually the case that they had a Christian friend. They had been quietly watching that person's life and priorities, and noticed that they were distinctive in their speech and behaviour. It was the godly life of the believer that led them to ask questions about their faith. We must encourage our young adults to seek to be godly at work, during their leisure activities and with their friends and neighbours, in both their actions and their words.

> IT WAS THE GODLY LIFE OF THE BELIEVER THAT LED THEM TO ASK QUESTIONS ABOUT THEIR FAITH.

Large-scale evangelistic events

From time to time – maybe three times a year – it is helpful to have a large evangelistic event that they can be encouraged to invite friends and colleagues to. Of course, there may be large-scale events happening across the wider church, but young adults are more likely to come when these have particular interest or relevance to them. There is a list of ideas for tried and tested events in Appendix 1.

YOUNG ADULTS ARE MORE LIKELY TO COME WHEN THESE HAVE PARTICULAR INTEREST OR RELEVANCE TO THEM.

I could tell many stories of how being invited to an event like this was someone's first contact with church.

Katy is a typical example. She came to a movie night at church, which led her to attend an evangelistic course. Then she started coming regularly to church on Sundays, gradually coming to the point where she called herself a believer.

Having an event does not replace the need for ongoing friendship evangelism, but it does give a focus to prayer. It is also encouraging when believers are all seeking to unite around a common goal of inviting people along.

Anne Hounsell, from my own church group, says:

> We often have guest events for the twenties to thirties which are a great way of inviting our friends to church. The young adults emphasis on evangelism has helped me be more distinctive for Christ in the workplace, encouraged me to witness to my family, and helped me on my journey to be more like Jesus.

Key ingredients of a good event

- Publicity – through church website and during services; perhaps use a colourful/professional-looking invite (we use 'iStock' photo on the Internet for images). Give out invitations at church to distribute among friends.
- Appeal to a wide range of people, especially young adults.
- Food and drink should be provided – a meal if possible, or nibbles.
- Make sure there are feedback forms asking people how they found the event (tick box) and if they want more information about evangelistic courses/future events at church/church services. Give space for email and postal address. Follow-up is essential.
- A friendly, welcoming atmosphere.
- A clear, engaging speaker who can explain the gospel in a light, relevant and jargon-free manner. Invite someone from another church if necessary.
- A well-organized event make people will feel comfortable and want to come back.
- A venue that is the right size for the number of people coming. A 'neutral' venue is better than a church building.
- An event that is free of charge (could have donation baskets, or ask church members to donate money to cover costs).

- Think about appropriate decorations. Make the venue look attractive, especially if a church building.
- What is your event feeding into? Offer something else they can come to – another evangelistic event, or a course that clearly and simply explains the gospel. If possible, time the event a week before the course.

NB: A variety of events over time will attract lots of different types of people.

Evangelistic courses

It is important to have a course to invite people to where they can be exposed to the person of Jesus through the pages of a Gospel. Its other purpose is to give them an opportunity to ask lots of questions, and express objections to faith in Jesus.

My church runs a course every term on a different Gospel. After a meal, there is a short talk and discussion around tables. These are organized according to age groups, which means that people have a chance to form meaningful friendships which helps them to keep coming. Occasionally my group has bonded so well that they have wanted to keep meeting long after the course has finished, and look at a different part of the Bible together.

IT IS IMPORTANT TO HAVE A COURSE TO INVITE PEOPLE TO WHERE THEY CAN BE EXPOSED TO THE PERSON OF JESUS THROUGH THE PAGES OF A GOSPEL.

If you can, advertise your course on the church website. One young couple who were getting married and wanted to find out more about Christianity found our church website, saw we were starting a course, and came along. They both gave their lives to Jesus at the end of the course.

Courses can be run in someone's home if the group is small. This will help it to feel more relaxed and informal. Watching a video is good, as it helps the non-believer to feel able to disagree with the speaker because he isn't present!

Resources for courses: There are a few good courses available. Check out www.10ofthose.com for suggestions.

Evangelism in small groups

Encouraging Bible study or friendship groups to organize smaller evangelistic events can be very fruitful. It also helps make Christians more focused in evangelism.

It benefits the small groups by resulting in greater:

- **Fellowship** – as we step out in faith together
- **Unity** – as we focus on a common goal and project
- **Prayer** – for our boldness, and each other's friends
- **Faith in God**, as we take risks
- **Confidence in the gospel**
- **Accountability towards each other**
- **Use of people's gifts** – working as a body
- **Ability to be outward-looking in focus and prayer**
- **Ease of follow-up**, as there are fewer people and strong relationships

Benefits for non-Christians

- They get to meet Christians in a social setting and make more friends.
- They get to see Christians relating to each other in community.
- They get a chance to ask the speaker questions.
- They get a chance to discuss with other people.
- They may have reservations about going into a church building.
- They may be intimidated by the idea of a big event.
- The talk and event can be more relevant to the non-believers present.
- They will be more likely to come to a church service after going to a smaller event first.

Benefits for our wider church mission

- It will bring new people to church services.
- It will bring people to evangelistic courses.
- It will bring new people into our groups.
- It will encourage us in our evangelism as a church.

Supporting young adults as they witness at work

As Christians we know the importance of sharing the gospel with others, but it can be something we just pay lip-service to. It's a different thing altogether on Monday morning, when we are meant to put this into practice.

Those who have recently graduated or have left school and found themselves in the bewildering and intimidating world of work need to be shown how to conduct themselves as Christians and how to begin to share their faith. It is a very different and much harder environment for evangelism than university or school. This difference can mean people never really witness at work. They need huge support, advice, encouragement and good role models from the wider congregation who can offer accountability and advice on how to get started in evangelism. There is nothing more encouraging than seeing someone more experienced who has been doing this for longer.

THERE IS NOTHING MORE ENCOURAGING THAN SEEING SOMEONE MORE EXPERIENCED WHO HAS BEEN DOING THIS FOR LONGER.

It will not be easy convincing people to share the gospel in their workplace. Here are some of the common reasons why they will find this difficult:

- **Fear of getting into trouble with their employer**
- **Fear of a lawsuit – if they work in the public sector**
- **Work is busy, and there isn't time for chatting**
- **Colleagues don't talk about personal issues or lives**
- **Colleagues are only acquaintances and not friends, therefore not keen to socialize after work**
- **Colleagues are all older, married, with families – nothing in common**
- **They don't feel able to answer people's questions**
- **They are the only Christian at work and want to fit in**

If people are unemployed, then we will be sensitive

about this. We can encourage them to be looking for opportunities to witness with people they see on a regular basis.

Some practical suggestions

- Encourage leaders to ask their small-group members to share prayer requests for non-Christians as regular practice.

- This will bring evangelism into the forum of the Bible study group and make evangelism among work colleagues a social norm – even if the idea is initially new or scary. One of the reasons why young adults don't share the gospel at work is because they are not praying for opportunities.

- Encourage group members to form prayer triplets (of the same gender) where they can pray weekly and more in-depth for unbelieving friends. These groups can also be accountability partners, where they ask each other how their evangelism at work is going.

- Interview older people seeking to witness in different fields of work.

- Invite The Christian Institute (www.christian.org.uk) or Christian Concern (www.christianconcern.com) to explain about the freedom and rights of sharing the gospel at work. This might clear confusion, and encourage those fearful of getting the sack.

- Encourage and help Christians to hold evangelistic events at work – carol services, evangelistic courses, one-off events discussing an issue.

- **Have a 'Gospel give-away'. Each Christian is given a copy of a Gospel and asked to carry it around with them at work, praying for opportunities for someone to give it to, and for a conversation. The fact that everyone is seeking to do this together can be very encouraging.**
- **Challenge them to read a Christian book and pass it on to someone at work.**

Some of the following titles may be helpful:

Rico Tice and Barry Cooper, *Christianity Explored* (Surrey: The Good Book Company, 2002).

Tim Keller, *Counterfeit Gods* (London: Hodder & Stoughton, 2009).

Roger Carswell, *Grill a Christian* (Chorley: 10Publishing, 2011).

Paul Williams and Barry Cooper, *If I Could Ask God One Question* (Surrey: The Good Book Company, 2007).

Graham Daniels, *My Mate's Gone Mad* (Milton Keynes: Authentic Media, 2007).

Mike Cain, *Real Life Jesus* (Nottingham: IVP, 2008).

DJ Carswell, *Real Lives* (Chorley: 10Publishing, 2012)

Lee Strobel, *The Case for Christ* (Grand Rapids, MI: Zondervan, 1998).

Tim Keller, *The Reason for God* (London: Hodder & Stoughton, 2008).

Amy Orr-Ewing, *Why Trust the Bible* (Nottingham, IVP, 2005).

NOTE
1. John Chapman, *Know and Tell the Gospel* (Kingsford, NSW: St Matthias Press, 1998).

CHAPTER 7:

Developing Community

Community is essential for Christian maturity, as Alison, a young woman of 30, testifies.

I became a Christian about five years ago through a Christianity Explored course, and started attending a twenties to thirties' group soon after. It has been a vital part of my Christian growth. Initially I was in a group with other new Christians, which was great as we were all at a similar stage. I felt comfortable in asking all kinds of questions, without feeling I was the only one who did not know the answers!

> I FELT COMFORTABLE IN ASKING ALL KINDS OF QUESTIONS, WITHOUT FEELING I WAS THE ONLY ONE WHO DID NOT KNOW THE ANSWERS!

As a newcomer in a large church, it can be quite difficult to get to know people. I sat next to different people every Sunday, and therefore did not really have an opportunity to build up relationships. Being able to chat over dinner and then study the Bible with a group of about ten people meant that it was much easier to get to know them. Also – given that we were all a similar age – we naturally had quite a lot in common, which again made forming friendships easier.

I had recently started work after university, as had many others. The majority were single, like me, and many lived in rented houses with house-mates – also like me. These may sound like small things, but they all made it easier to connect. It also meant we had more time to spend with each other outside church. I found this really important in consolidating friendships, which then helped me to be more honest with others in my group about any struggles, which they also had. This made applying the Bible passage to our lives more powerful, because we could help each other work through any issues.

Community: A mixed blessing?

Community isn't an optional extra for extroverts, but a God-given blessing to all believers.

When we were reconciled into relationship with God, our heavenly Father, we also entered into relationship with a family of believers. We are brothers and sisters, a community of sinners saved by grace, looking forward together to our great inheritance in heaven.

This new community is one of the privileges of being a believer, but it doesn't always feel like a blessing. Our experience is often one of frustration, disappointment and fragile relationships.

The Bible is realistic about how difficult church life can be: 'What causes fights and quarrels among you? Don't they come from your desires that battle within you? You want something but don't get it. You kill and covet, but you cannot have what you want. You quarrel and fight' (Jas. 4:1,2).

Community will fail when we are all living as individuals – looking after the needs of number one rather than being other-person centred. Paul writes to the church at Philippi: 'Do nothing out of selfish ambition or vain conceit, but in humility consider others better than yourselves' (2:3).

The New Testament gives us some very practical advice about things which destroy community. We would do well to heed these warnings:

- **'Therefore let us stop passing judgment on one another' (Rom. 14:13).**

- **'If you keep on biting and devouring each other, watch out or you will be destroyed by each other' (Gal. 5:15).**

- **'Let us not become conceited, provoking and envying each other' (Gal. 5:26).**

We are to live differently from the world around us, because we are different. We are children of our heavenly Father, and are called to grow in the family likeness. God is very concerned with how His children treat one another: 'Therefore, as God's chosen people, holy and dearly loved, clothe yourselves with compassion, kindness, humility, gentleness and patience. Bear with each other and forgive whatever grievances you may have against one another. Forgive as the Lord forgave you. And over all these virtues put on love, which binds them all together in perfect unity' (Col. 3:12–14).

Serving one another in love

What does it look like in practice to serve and love one another? The New Testament has some very helpful instructions on how to build community.

- '. . . be mutually encouraged by each other's faith' (Rom. 1:12).

- '. . . make every effort to do what leads to peace and to mutual edification' (Rom. 14:19).

- '. . . encourage one another daily . . . so that none of you will be hardened by sin's deceitfulness' (Heb. 3:13).

Building community

John Hindley from Broadgrace Church, Norfolk, has planted two churches. He shares his experience of encouraging community to form.

Only the Spirit can build us into community as Christians, but we can walk in step with Him, or grieve Him. These are the blocks I have tried to put in place to live out the community life we have as a gift in Christ.

Word and prayer: As community is the work of the Spirit, the faithful teaching of the Word of Christ is essential. This is the sword of the Spirit that Jesus wields to cut out our coldness and individualism and to bind us together in love.

Time: If church is a community, a family, we need to hang out together. This means paring back organized activities, that coffee and cake is part of the Sunday meeting in reality. It means making sure people don't see church as a chore, but as a joy. It means lots of coffees, pints, meals, and just hanging out together.

Honesty: We need to be real, which means we need to be able to confess our sins to one another. So much Christian culture is pharisaic. This has put a huge onus on me as a pastor. If my real accountability, honest Christian friends, people I relax with, are outside my church, then I am making what I teach a lie and making Christ out to be a liar. If God is trinity and He makes us like Him and I am not open with my church family as real brothers and sisters, then I am simply a hypocrite.

> LOVE IS A MOVEMENT OF THE HEART, AND I CAN NO MORE CHANGE MY HEART THAN CARVE FLINT WITH MY WILLPOWER.

Love: We need to love each other. And I can't make anyone love anyone else, because I can't make myself love anyone. I can make myself be nice to people, but love them? No way! Love is a movement of the heart, and I can no more change my heart than carve flint with my willpower. So we are back to the Spirit, back to prayer, and back to seeing the glory of Christ in His Word and so being transformed to be like Him.

The Revd Andrew Dunlop, former curate of St Andrews, Plymouth, says:

> My philosophy of twenties and thirties' groups is that there needs to be plenty of time to chat, mingle

and hang out – after all, single people really want to get to know others for community, friendship, and the possibility of meeting a partner. However, a group which is purely social will not last too long. It needs a point. So we decided to offer them two things:

1. To continue with regular social events, but less often. These were open to anyone, in the church or not, and were easy to invite friends to. These included a trip to the Eden Project, a photo scavenger hunt, pancake parties, and a photo competition at a National Trust property.

2. An evening group specifically for young adults – like a largish small group. Each week we ate a meal together (taking it in turns to cook something simple), and had a discussion or Bible study afterwards, with time for prayer. We grouped them into prayer triplets to offer consistency and accountability (they got a say in who they went with).

Overall I think it really helped some people to come into the church in a bigger way than they might have otherwise.

As we have seen, it's a challenge to foster a sense of community among a large group, but not impossible. There are several things that can help. Some churches use name labels to aid poor memories, or have a church directory with photos and addresses.

Here are some ideas that churches have done across the country, either for just young adults or for the whole church.

Sports day. Tournaments of five-a-side football, badminton, volleyball, tennis and a barbecue.

Church picnic. Members bring food to share; there can be sports activities, tug-of-war, face painting, bouncy castle.

Guess who's coming for dinner. Church members offer to host dinners for four to eight people, and the church office assigns random members to hosts, mixing up people from their usual groups. This could happen three to four times a year.

Brunches and topical teaching – for men or women.

Days away. A day of teaching on a topic with lunch included.

Weekend away. Once or twice a year. This is a real opportunity for building community/relationships, and a chance to do some extra topical teaching.

Book discussion groups. To meet once every two months or so to discuss a Christian book.

Meals. Small groups hosting a lunch/dinner for another small group.

Team dinners. If there is a team of leaders, have a dinner together three times a year to foster fellowship.

Integrating newcomers

- Give them a card to get contact details.
- Send an information pack with all relevant information about the church.
- Invite all newcomers to come to a welcome dinner before they commit to becoming members. The meal and talk by the church leader helps them to decide

whether they want to commit to the vision and ethos of the church.

- Assign each newcomer a more established member to befriend and introduce them to people.
- Meet them on their own to talk about their previous church, service, and reason for moving church.

Belonging Course

The Belonging Course is a three-night course that I came across when I was in Sydney, at the Church by the Bridge. It is run by the minister and his wife in their home, three times a year.

Week 1: Belonging to Jesus and the church – what does it mean, and why belong to a church? They look at key Bible passages about following Jesus and the importance of committing to church.

Week 2: Living for Jesus – this outlines the vision of the church and the importance of the Bible, prayer and fellowship, attending a regular service, belonging to a Bible study group, having Quiet Times, attending church prayer meetings, praying for the church.

Week 3: Loving like Jesus – this looks at the mission of the church, locally and worldwide, introducing its mission partners. Loving Jesus means loving the church family – generosity in giving and serving the church. They also highlight ways to be involved and serve. In this session, expectations of church members are made clear and, in turn, what they can expect from the leaders.

This course not only grounds people in what church membership looks like, but also quickly helps them see if this is something they want to commit to. The course fosters a sense of community between newcomers, and helps to establish a relationship with the minister.

Attracting non-Christians

Seek to be a community that is outward-looking, that welcomes non-Christians. Some people are looking for a group to belong to, and are attracted to the Christian community. We have non-believers who attend small groups and weekends away long before they commit to following Jesus. It is great that they feel welcome to come along and learn about the gospel as they get to know Christian believers.

Small-group community

If the group is very large, community is difficult because people don't really know each other. This is one of the reasons why small-group Bible studies exist. It is easier to demonstrate and build community with a group of eight to ten people.

CHRISTIAN COMMUNITY AND RELATIONSHIPS IN THE BIBLE ARE ALWAYS IN THE CONTEXT OF BIBLE STUDY AND PRAYER.

Christian community and relationships in the Bible are always in the context of Bible study and prayer. These are the most helpful in growing in spiritual maturity.

One young man shares how he has benefited from his small-group community:

> Fellowship with other Christians in my age group has been incredibly important for me. I have met some of my closest and wisest friends here, and over the years have been able to help them through the ups and downs of their faith, as they are now helping me. To make and develop friendships with Christians of the same age in the same career . . . with the same interests, and therefore ultimately having the same struggles and temptations, has often been a huge encouragement as I seek to live for Jesus. (J.D., age 27)

Practical ways to help build a strong community within a small group

Setting up the group

- Start with a meal together to begin the process of relationship-building.
- Go through New Testament passages – what should Christian community look like?
- Discuss what this looks like during the study, and outside study time.
- Commit to praying for each other throughout the week, and having group confidentiality.
- Share previous experiences/lessons of good and bad examples of group.
- Swap email addresses and phone numbers.

- Set expectations for the members about commitment and attendance; for example, sending apologies if unable to come.

- Consider having a group agreement or covenant that everyone signs.

- Plan a series of regular socials. Agree on dates at the beginning of the term.

- Discuss what you are going to study together, and what you hope to gain from it.

- Encourage group discussion, questions and every-member participation.

- Find out everyone's birthdays, mark with a card and cake from the group.

- Discuss start and end times so that everyone's circumstances are taken into account.

- Agree on a venue and time that is accessible to all; arrange lifts if necessary.

- Discuss parking in advance.

- Make an agreement to have mobile phones off or on silent.

Before the study

- Arrange the room so everyone can see each other. Eye contact aids discussion.

- Make sure lighting and heating is comfortable and not distracting.

- Ensure people get a friendly welcome as they arrive.
- Start with a drink and something to eat to help people relax.
- Ask how their week is going.
- Have an ice-breaker question or activity to help the group get to know each other. Check out, for example, *300+ Sizzling Ice-breakers* by Michael Puffett with Blair Mundell (Oxford: Monarch Books, 2009).
- Take turns each week to share your testimony.
- Pray for concentration and wisdom.

During the study
- Try to involve everyone.
- Remember, ensure you have eye contact with everyone.
- Validate and encourage when people contribute.
- Do occasional work in pairs, to include quieter people.
- Seek to draw people out and involve them.
- Watch their body language.
- Be aware of the passage raising sensitive issues of application for group members.
- Encourage honesty in application – model vulnerability.
- Apply the passage directly to situations group members are facing.
- Aim to finish with enough time for prayer.

The prayer time

- Try different formats each week for variety to suit different people.
- In advance, ask different members of the group to plan the prayer time.
- Pray for each other's unbelieving friends and witness at work.
- Have someone make notes and email them out to the group.
- Share something from the passage to pray for, as well as something personal.
- Encourage group accountability with the issues people have discussed.
- Keep an eye on the time, limit number of prayer points per person.
- If running out of time, share and pray in twos and threes.
- Adopt a mission partner to pray for as a group.
- Model being vulnerable in prayer.

After the prayer time

- Make sure everyone has a lift home.
- Offer more refreshments.
- Encourage people to stay and chat if they can.
- Remind the group to keep praying for each other through the week.

Outside group time

- Keep in touch by phone, text or email.
- Pray for each other.
- Offer hospitality.
- Shop for people if they are sick.
- Call someone if they missed the group.
- Socialize together.
- Lend each other possessions, e.g. books.

The role of the small-group leader in building community

Read these words of wisdom by Katherine Monument from St Andrew the Great, Cambridge. She has been a small-group leader for many years.

> When creating a community in a twenties to thirties' Bible study group, there are a few key principles to establish.

> **Facilitate:** You shouldn't underestimate the importance of facilitating interactions within the group before, during and post-Bible study – as well as socially for coffee, dinner, or whatever. Small things matter – like introducing people, remembering key details about them, 'hosting' conversations, helping group members to start friendships.

SMALL THINGS MATTER – LIKE INTRODUCING PEOPLE, REMEMBERING KEY DETAILS ABOUT THEM.

Members come with different expectations and wishes in terms of what they want to invest. Some want the group to be an acquaintance-level Bible study group, nothing more. They leave on time at the end, and have no desire to invest in deep friendships; they have those needs met elsewhere.

Others, however, want the group to be their main social group and support system, especially if they are new to the town or church. Different groups require different degrees of help in facilitating friendships and discussions. As a leader, you have to read the situation and pitch it accordingly.

Connect: It is vital to connect with people in a real sense. This can help to foster a sense of community and openness within the group. This can be achieved by setting the tone in terms of what you share as a leader. As much as is appropriate, try to be real and honest (obviously not things that are too personal or inappropriate – keep those for a trusted inner circle of Christian friends). Share what is hard and what you are thankful for; don't be afraid not to have all the answers. This gives permission for others to say what they are finding hard. The group is then far more likely to invest emotionally. We often ask group members to share very personal prayer requests. Initially, this is effectively with a group of strangers, but as leaders we can help to build up bonds of trust by sharing truthfully.

> SHARE WHAT IS HARD AND WHAT YOU ARE THANKFUL FOR; DON'T BE AFRAID NOT TO HAVE ALL THE ANSWERS.

Support: Meeting up with group members regularly

and introducing them to other friends/connections within and outside of church can help people feel part of a community quickly. Walk alongside them – find a shared interest (e.g. football), meet up to watch a match and chat about it over a drink. This will lead to real connections being made. Meeting up for a quick pre-church coffee can help to keep your finger on the pulse of how they are doing in their faith and in life in general. That way, you can really support them because you know what is really going on.

CHAPTER 8:

Pastoral Care

Life changes

As I head towards my late thirties, I'm reflecting on all the life changes and big decisions I have made since leaving university – four job changes to adjust to, four new places where I didn't know anyone, six different house-mates, five new churches to settle into, two relationship break-ups, decisions about getting married, whether or not to buy a house.

All of this partly comes with the territory of growing up, but there are lots of major life changes and stressful decisions to make in your twenties and thirties. Some get married and have children for the first time, some are dealing with health problems, threats of redundancy, financial worries, squabbles with house-mates, struggling with singleness, or with a difficult marriage.

THERE ARE LOTS OF MAJOR LIFE CHANGES AND STRESSFUL DECISIONS TO MAKE IN YOUR TWENTIES AND THIRTIES.

People in this age group need lots of care and support – both from more mature Christians, and from a structure where they can meet with their peers and care for each other.

What is pastoral care?

Pastoral care is given by someone who helps you understand God's Word in the context of personal friendship. It is not the same as counselling.

Counselling and pastoral care have different aims and methods:

- **The goal in counselling is happiness, but the goal in pastoral care is holiness.**
- **The perceived problem in counselling is sickness, but in pastoral care it is sin.**
- **The method in counselling is listening and asking questions; pastoral care also corrects us, but from the Bible.**
- **The level of involvement will be a professional distance in counselling, but tears and love are appropriate in pastoral care.**
- **In counselling self-help is encouraged, but pastoral care points us to the Holy Spirit's help.**
- **In counselling our only source of guidance is from our experience, but pastoral care will encourage us to pray and read Scripture.**
- **In counselling there is a need for a trained expert, whereas in pastoral care all you need is a godly, mature Christian.**

Men and women

Men and women struggle with different issues, although there is some overlap. Below, I have outlined some of the most common issues that young Christian adults want to discuss:

Women

Self-doubt, low self-esteem, image, depression, self-harming, eating disorders, same-sex attraction, feeling suicidal, singleness, dating an unbeliever, an argument with a female friend, should they marry or break up with boyfriend, stress at work, doubts about the gospel, parental problems.

Our male pastoral staff has identified these as the most common issues among young male adults:

Men

Identity – how to be a man, boyfriend or husband; homosexuality, sex, pornography and masturbation. Singleness, depression (often relating to feelings of purposelessness), handling money, self-discipline, spiritual responsibilities, work. There can also be a range of psychiatric conditions, from everything on the autistic spectrum to personality disorders. Plus issues regarding self-harm, substance abuse, including alcohol, drugs, performance-enhancing drugs, divorce/affairs, bulimia, and anorexia.

Unspoken issues

I conducted an anonymous survey among 354 Christians in their twenties and thirties. I asked which issues they found hard to discuss with church leaders. Many are struggling in silence, without any pastoral support.

The results

Pornography: 25

Masturbation: 12

Lust: 44

Doubt: 28

Sexual purity (actions): 28

Excessive alcohol: 6

Singleness: 25

Depression: 20

Loneliness: 14

Marital issues: 14

Eating disorders: 7

Lack of Quiet Times: 10

Jealousy: 15

Same-sex attraction: 7

Self-harming: 1

Debt: 4

Breaking the silence

If we are aware of the issues that people are quietly wrestling with, one way to bring them out into the open is in a public forum. References to these could be made in sermon application, Bible studies, and could be questions to ask in accountability relationships and prayer triplets. If these issues were talked about more openly as a common struggle, then our young adults wouldn't be so reluctant to share their own personal battle. If they are willing to discuss these things with church pastoral staff, they are more likely to be supported.

Addictions

Struggles with issues such as pornography and masturbation are actually addictions. Being told to simply stop is not enough. Much prayer, Christian support and accountability is needed to overcome an addiction. It will take time, and the transformation will be unlikely to happen overnight. Two helpful books on this are: *Addictions* by Edward Welch (New Jersey: P&R Publishing, 2001) and *You Can Change* by Tim Chester (Leicester: IVP, 2008).

Pornography

This battle has become more common over the last ten years, with the accessibility of the Internet on gadgets and the increase of available porn sites. Our culture seems to be more open about watching pornography; it has become a social norm among non-Christians, who chat about it openly.

Many Christian singles, especially in their thirties, are curious and desperate to have sex. Some of it is just hormonal. They are not sure what to do with those longings and pornography satisfies a need, at least temporarily. Pornography often leads to masturbation and fuels a lustful heart. It makes sex into an idol, rather than a gift from God to be enjoyed in its proper context of marriage. Pornography reduces sex to an animalistic, physical act divorced from feelings, commitment or responsibility. Those who have been addicted as a single person can sometimes struggle to have sexual relations with their spouse. Our sin always has consequences.

Here is one single man's reflection on why he watches porn:

> As a single man in his thirties with raging hormones, it is very difficult not to look at a beautiful girl and wonder what she looks like naked. Pornography takes away the mystery, and gives you the chance to see naked women.
>
> A sexy girl advert pops up when you are surfing the web, and then pornography is one click away. It's a relief from sexual frustration, escapism from a difficult day at work. It usually leads to masturbation, and there is a great chemical relief immediately afterwards. Satisfying yourself after a hard day becomes an addictive habit. It's not long before the guilt and shame kick in, and I start to hate myself for my lack of self-control. I feel like the only one struggling with this double life.
>
> **IT'S NOT LONG BEFORE THE GUILT AND SHAME KICK IN, AND I START TO HATE MYSELF FOR MY LACK OF SELF-CONTROL.**
>
> I remember once driving to church shortly after looking at pornography. I couldn't face going in, so I turned the car round and came back home, racked with guilt and shame. The images stay ingrained on your memory for ages, and it's hard to think about anything else.
>
> I have found support and accountability with a group of male Christian friends. This is a great help, as this can be a taboo topic at church and never spoken about. I wish the preacher would talk about it, as I fear that if I tell someone I am struggling with pornography I will not be accepted at church.

Depression

On 11 June 2010, *The Guardian* reported that in the last decade, the number of anti-depressants prescribed by the NHS has almost doubled. In England in 2009, 39.1 million prescriptions were issued to help tackle depression, compared with 20.1 in 1999 in ten years. That is an increase of 95 per cent. Christians are not immune from depression, and in my experience it is extremely common among young adults. Here is Jenny's personal reflection on depression. She is a Christian, aged 30.

I have had depression on and off for nearly ten years. It affects all aspects of my life. At its worst, I really struggle to get out of bed. Sleeping/hiding in bed is easier than having to face life. When I feel low, I struggle to do normal things; this fuels my feeling of unworthiness and worsens my mood (especially if I have to cancel an event where I was going to help someone with something). I feel useless and rubbish, that no one really likes me – even God.

I start getting paranoid about things – for example, if someone doesn't reply to my text, that means they are cross with me or don't like me.

At its extreme, I have thought it would be better if I was not alive because then I wouldn't be a burden to anyone. I have had suicidal thoughts on several occasions, with one quite serious attempt early on.

At that point I felt I was not meant to be alive any more. All these negative thought cycles feed into each other and make things worse. I also engaged in a variety of destructive behaviours in an attempt to feel better and mask the pain I was feeling.

My lack of interest and motivation means doing things socially can be very difficult. This includes getting to church and Bible studies. Avoiding these things means I don't have to pretend I am interested or that I am 'fine'; I don't have to make the effort of talking to people. I can't concentrate anyway, and feel I have nothing useful to say.

The longer I am away from church, the more nervous I am to go back. I feel self-conscious, and that everyone would look at me or be talking about me. My depression also really affects my personal faith at home. It is very difficult to get the energy or enthusiasm to read the Bible or pray, and my mind feels dulled and lacking in concentration. If I am able to read the Bible, it needs to be a short section that I know quite well. I feel totally uninterested in God, that my depression is too difficult a problem for God to deal with and I just have to cope with it myself. I hope I will turn back to God when I am feeling better.

Self-harming

Sometimes this is a way of finding relief from depression, and the two are often connected. Here is an honest account from Elspeth, a Christian who is prone to self-harming when things get tough.

I started self-harming when I was 21. I had just started a new course at university, as well as experiencing a number of other changes, and was struggling to settle in. I started feeling anxious, low, and found it hard to concentrate. I started feeling really tense and agitated about things, but didn't know why. I couldn't explain my feelings to friends and thought they wouldn't understand anyway.

Cutting myself eased the tension straight away. The pain it caused and seeing the blood was an expression of the pain I felt on the inside. Turning the emotional pain into something visible seemed to help, but the tension release didn't last long. Then I would feel annoyed with myself and start to hate myself more. I used razors, blades, knifes or scissors to cut myself with. I also sometimes scratched my arm a lot so it would bleed, or pinch myself hard. It needed to be painful, ideally to break the skin and cause bleeding. As it went on, I would cut myself in places which I could hide, so no one would notice. I felt that most people would not understand and I did not want to worry my family.

IT FELT ALMOST HARDER TO TELL PEOPLE AT CHURCH BECAUSE I THOUGHT THEY WOULD LOOK DOWN ON ME, OR THINK I WAS A 'BAD' OR 'IMMATURE' CHRISTIAN.

It felt almost harder to tell people at church because I thought they would look down on me, or think I was a 'bad' or 'immature' Christian. Although I have talked about it with close friends, I don't think I was self-harming to seek attention. It was mainly to release my inner tension, something I felt that I could 'do' to make me feel better. I felt it was the one aspect of life I could control. That didn't last long, and I found myself doing it again and again. It was compulsive. Once I started thinking about it, the tension rose even more and I couldn't think about anything else until I self-harmed.

The other thing is that it turned into a habit. Even when my depression started to lift, often when I felt insecure/low/anxious, I would cut myself. I had learned that it made me feel better (if only temporarily), and was like a safety blanket. Even when I talked with my counsellor about less destructive ways of releasing tension, I still kept a box of blades under my bed in case I needed them. They made me feel safer.

Eating disorders

This is one Christian girl's experience. Rebecca is married, and in her twenties.

With hindsight, I've had a disordered relationship with food since I was around 15. This took the form of getting a kick out of being able to skip meals if I wanted. It happened fairly infrequently, and I tried to keep it secret. When I started university I gained weight in my first year – reaching a healthy weight for my height for the first time in ages – but can vividly recall a day that summer when I felt very fat and thought, 'I need to lose weight.'

I can't remember actively trying to lose lots by that point, but the thought took root. Over the next two years at university I gradually became more and more aware of what others were eating, how much I was eating, and how the two compared. Certainly by my final year I was exercising a lot – but loving it – and restricting what I was eating, so I was having (to the best of my knowledge) less than others around me. I also loved the feeling that came from that.

It was during a check-up with my GP when my periods stopped that she diagnosed anorexia nervosa, and the long process of NHS waiting lists for treatment began. While not blaming the very long wait I had between being diagnosed and eventually starting treatment (two years), things very quickly got very out of control. This was ironic, given that I had a feeling of being very much 'in control' when I was practising these disordered behaviours. That's part of the addiction; what starts off as fairly infrequent breaking from the norms regarding food and what most people do with it, very easily becomes the norm for you. You gradually become desensitized to thinking that you have any sort of problem. Eventually, my daily routine involved maximum amounts of exercise that I could reasonably fit in without being exhausted or others thinking something was wrong, coupled with a restricted diet. Calorie counting, restricting my intake, exercising and eating less than others became my focus. I was driven to succeed in these areas, and had meltdowns when I couldn't.

The cycle became self-perpetuating: I felt in control if I was doing these things, and was driven to do them more if other things were stressful, e.g. work (which it was), family life (which it was). However, doing them more made me more dependent on them as I'd panic if my routines were upset. I clearly remember leaving a friend's dinner party early because I couldn't cope that my fiancé . . . hadn't had the dessert I'd expected. I cycled home in floods of tears.

The underlying emotions that drive, fuel and maintain these behaviours are fear, anxiety and unfamiliarity. All express a need for control – for things to happen a certain way, and an extreme fear of a lack of control. On one hand, I know it's irrational; I know logically nothing bad can happen simply because I've eaten more than someone sitting next to me, or because the number on the scales says something I've arbitrarily decided is too much.

NO ONE TELLS YOU AT THE TIME THAT RESTRICTION/OVER-EXERCISING IS NOT A LONG-TERM ANSWER; YOU FIND OUT THE HARD WAY.

On the other hand, this whole thing has taken on a mind of its own (that makes sense, given it's a mental illness), and so, more often than not, it all seems entirely plausible, reasonable, logical. The addiction to these behaviours comes through simply finding they work short term but failing, at the time, to see that they are only a short-term 'solution'. Consequently, if they work once, they get used the next time and so dependency kicks in. It's like a caffeine addiction, only worse. No one tells you at the time that restriction/over-exercising is not a long-term answer; you find out the hard way. Engaging in these behaviours is attractive because it makes you feel in control; superior; better than others; that you can achieve something that other people can't. It becomes 'your thing' and you don't want it to be taken away.

I don't want to give the impression that it was *never* motivated by a desire to be thinner – partly it was ... but that motivation quickly became overshadowed by all others, until the whole thing became 'normal' and almost subconscious.

In summary, in the beginning the entire illness gives the impression of providing answers and solutions to problems without making you aware that that's what you are using the behaviours for. This is why it's cunning and deceptive. Our minds are powerful things – but not just for good. What I thought I was controlling has ended up controlling me, and this is something that I still am blinded to quite a lot of the time. I'm being helped by Cognitive Behaviour Therapy at my local hospital, and have a supportive GP who I see regularly, but the recovery process is long and slow. The illness is illogical, and cannot be undone with a logical voice telling you to 'eat more'. It takes more than that.

OUR MINDS ARE POWERFUL THINGS – BUT NOT JUST FOR GOOD. WHAT I THOUGHT I WAS CONTROLLING HAS ENDED UP CONTROLLING ME.

One thing I've failed to do throughout almost all the early stages is to pray about it. I didn't regularly take the issues causing me anxiety to God in prayer, nor did I take any self-esteem issues there either. Instead, I misused and abused good things he had given me. I'm still learning to see how all of this is a means of self-justification and a way of taking matters into my own hands. I can't do that – only God can justify, and only God can control. The damage is done now and with His gracious help I hope He will help me reverse things and become more like the person He created me to be.

Singleness

This is a very painful issue for many young adults. Some desperately want to get married and have children, but haven't met anyone suitable. Increasingly, there are more single women than men in churches, so inevitably some will remain single.

Churches are well set up for couples and families, but often singles feel neglected or just 'used'. We need to make sure our language and activities don't assume people are in couples, nor make singles feel they are less valued or to be pitied. The apostle Paul was extremely positive about the gift of singleness, and we need to help our singles to feel content in Christ and to feel a valued part of the church family.

Here is Lucy's reflection of being single, aged 38.

It was always my life's dream to get married and have children, but it hasn't happened to me yet. I sometimes wonder why God is punishing me by withholding this gift. If I'm not blaming God, then I blame myself and think the problem must lie with me. I must be very unattractive and undesirable, even though I do my best to look nice. I struggle with envy when I see my friends so happy with their husbands, and long to have that kind of intimacy with someone who accepts me as I am. I used to go on holiday and meet up with my friends, but they are too busy now with their families. I find friendships with people twelve years younger, because they are single like me, and have time to spare. Sometimes church is too painful, seeing all the young parents with babies and knowing that time is running out for me. Of course, I try to keep busy, serve where I can, try to keep smiling, but the ache within my heart never goes away. When I'm alone at night, the tears start to flow.

Doubt

In a world where absolute truth is attacked and the authority of the Bible is continually undermined, it is not surprising that this causes our young adults to doubt its truths from time to time. We need to allow them to express such doubts, equip them with the tools to confront them and support them patiently in the process.

An honest reflection

I have been attending the twenties to thirties' group for almost five years. During that time I have developed and matured as a Christian in many ways, although I am presently experiencing some large and rather painful doubts in my faith. Through lessons learned, I am seeking to trust in God rather than turn away from Him. I am seeking to read more of His Word to encourage and challenge my doubts. I have a better understanding that having doubts is part of the Christian's walk; that Jesus fully accepts us as the doubting, weak sinners that we are, not as the strong, formidable 'super-Christians' we feel we should be. I only need to look at Jesus' treatment of Thomas for evidence of this.

Through the twenties to thirties' group, I have learned that there is nothing I can do to make myself right in God's eyes. Rather, it is all through what Jesus has done. In our egocentric, technology-filled, can-do Western culture, that message has never been more countercultural or important.

The two elements which have affected me the most are the weekly Bible studies and fellowship with other Christians in my age group. Meeting weekly to read God's Word in the Bible, study its message, and consider how we can apply it to our twenty-first century lives, has really helped transform my Christian life. There is still a long way for me to go, but my understanding of the Bible has really matured since attending the group. It is a real testament to this ministry that during this difficult time in my walk with God, my key instinct is to turn towards the Bible and try to cling onto the promises within it, as opposed to just giving up. Having spent five years learning more about the love and faithfulness of God and His Son, Jesus, I want to have a stronger faith . . . As I seek to confront and challenge my current doubts (and no doubt future ones along the way), I know that my strongest weapons will be my faith in God, however weak it may currently feel, my reading about His character

THROUGH THE TWENTIES TO THIRTIES' GROUP, I HAVE LEARNED THAT THERE IS NOTHING I CAN DO TO MAKE MYSELF RIGHT IN GOD'S EYES.

in His Word, and the daily witness of friends who I can confide in and rely on to be praying for me. One day it might be them needing me in return. The young adult group has been instrumental in developing all three of these, and I know that I would be a much more immature Christian without it. (James, age 27)

How can we help as a church?

In general, we can work hard at community and building loving relationships where people feel accepted and able to share their issues. We need to train small-group leaders in pastoral care, so there are people in place to talk to about their problems. Encouraging and helping to set up prayer triplets will give people an opportunity for weekly support and accountability. We also need well-applied Bible teaching in sermons, and small groups that are real and open about the struggles people face.

Having occasional talks about some of the unspoken issues covered in this chapter will give everyone a better understanding and idea of how to support friends who are wrestling with these problems.

We should also encourage everyone to serve with an other-person centred attitude.

Role of the small-group leader

- **Developing trust and regular accountability with**

group members of the same sex.

- Modelling a godly life with gospel priorities, openness about struggles.
- Teaching grace through Bible studies and in conversation.
- Providing friendship and hospitality with group members.
- Giving pastoral support, and discipling of group members.
- Motivating group members to be fully involved and committed to serving the church.
- Modelling handling of the Bible with well-applied Bible studies.
- Being committed in prayer for the spiritual growth of the members of the group.

Struggling with same-sex attraction

Our church invited the True Freedom Trust to give a talk to students about same-sex attraction. The speaker was a mature male Christian who had struggled with this for a long time. This was well attended.

Afterwards we launched a group for those struggling in this area. They meet several times a year and discuss relevant articles and books, look at the Bible together, and pray. By providing a support group, we are recognizing an issue that several struggle with, and are giving them a framework in which to deal with it biblically and helpfully.

The group is anonymous and confidential except for the involvement of one church leader who helps to steer the group.

The True Freedom Trust produces literature, provides speakers, and are a great network of support (http://truefreedomtrust.co.uk).

Helpful books on this subject:

Alex Tylee, *Walking with Gay Friends* (Nottingham: IVP, 2007).

Wesley Hill, *Washed and Waiting* (Grand Rapids, MI: Zondervan, 2010).

Christopher Keane, *What Some of You Were* (Kingsford, NSW: Matthias Media, 2001).

Struggling with pornography

There is no reason why there couldn't be a similar group for people wrestling with this subject. We also had a talk about this issue for all young adults. Having an extra, optional talk will keep people away for fear of being 'found out'. It is something that both genders struggle with, but churches sometimes wrongly assume it's just a male issue. There are accountability computer programmes available, such as 'Covenant Eyes', which allow someone else to see which Internet sites you have visited over a month. This is a wonderful deterrent, if only people are willing to admit this issue is a temptation.

Helpful books on the subject:

Tim Chester, *Captured by a Better Vision* (Nottingham: IVP, 2010).

Stephen Arterburn, Fred Stoeker, *Every Man's Battle: Winning the War on Sexual Temptation* (NY: Doubleday Religious Publishing Group, 2009).

Shannon Ethridge, *Every Woman's Battle* (Colorado Springs, CO: WaterBrook Press, 2003).

Paul Grimmond, *Purity in the Age of Porn* (Kingsford, NSW: Matthias Media, 2009).

Joshua Harris, *Sex is Not the Problem (Lust is)* (Colorado Springs, CO: Multnomah Books, 2005).

CHAPTER 9:

Ready to Serve

A life-changing decision

Each week Tony sat in the same place with the same people. He had been doing the same thing for the last seven years, since leaving university. He liked being under the radar, observing what was going on around him. There were others better suited to serve and lead, and besides, he was too busy. He had two good friends to sit with; he didn't need any new friends at church. He was comfortable with the way it was.

Then something happened to unsettle his peace. A church plant was taking place. Lots of Bible study leaders were going, and there were gaps to be filled. Suddenly he was being asked to help lead – no experience needed, training would be given.

> HE LIKED BEING UNDER THE RADAR. THERE WERE OTHERS BETTER SUITED TO SERVE AND LEAD, AND BESIDES, HE WAS TOO BUSY.

Tony racked his brain for a good excuse, but they all sounded weak and selfish. He reluctantly volunteered for the Bible study leader training.

This decision certainly helped the church, but now – years later – Tony says that decision changed his life. He became an able and competent Bible study leader and discovered he was actually well suited to the role. He even found it fulfilling.

He met new people, some of whom became good friends. Church had new purpose and excitement for him. He bought a big dining room table and learned to cook, so he could have his group over for dinner. He grew spiritually as he studied the Bible study passage for himself each week. He also met his wife – one of the other leaders.

Yes, serving the church was the best decision Tony ever made.

Bodybuilding

This true story is one of many I could have told. God has designed us for service, and when we give ourselves to serving others we truly find ourselves.

Are you into bodybuilding? Each week I go to the gym and see men spending great time and effort building up their bodies and strengthening their muscles. This is what we need to be doing in our churches – getting fit and strong for service.

In Ephesians 4:11–13, Paul uses the metaphor of the body to describe the church. God has given 'personal trainers' to build up the body (apostles and prophets, and now evangelists, pastors and teachers). These personal trainers have one goal: to prepare the body for works of service.

The reason? To build up the whole body to become united and mature in Christ – the head.

This passage shows that if we want a united, mature and strong church then we all need to be serving. It's not just for the minister or church staff, and it's not just for the mature and 'keenies'! Paul says we serve in order to become keen and mature, not wait until we are. This is what Tony discovered when he reluctantly started serving.

Every member ministry

Some people like to think of church as a bus. The minister is the driver and is steering the bus along the direction they want to go. The rest are passengers, passively enjoying the ride, confident in the driver's skill to take them to their destination. In some ways this is a pleasant picture, and one that appeals to our longing for ease and comfort.

If you were to ask young adults about this idea, it would appeal to many. They are a generation of consumers, and church can too easily become just another commodity that is there to meet their needs. Sometimes churches have people in their twenties and thirties, but all they do each week is sit in a clique together at the back, and go to the pub afterwards for a drink. They don't really engage with the rest of the church, and there seems little benefit from them being there.

However, the bus metaphor is not a biblical model for the church – it couldn't be further away from God's plan, as expressed in Ephesians 4. The church is more like an Oxbridge rowing boat with the cox shouting directions and looking ahead, while every member of the crew works hard and pulls together as one team.

AS EACH NEW PERSON EMBARKS UPON SERVICE, THE CHURCH WILL GROW AND BE BUILT UP.

'Every member ministry' – some churches have this statement as part of their vision. This is a great way of expressing the truths of Ephesians 4. We are all needed as various parts of the body to serve and use our God-given gifts and abilities. This is the only way for the church to grow and for each muscle (person) to be strengthened. As each new person embarks upon service, the church will grow and be built up. What a great vision to have for your church and your young adults!

Discovering and using our gifts

Some may claim they cannot serve because they have no gifts. We need to encourage them from this Scripture that every member of the body can serve, and should.

In fact, most of us only discover our God-given gifts through serving others. Sometimes we need the help of the wider Christian family to help us discover what our gifts are. Asking an older, wiser Christian who knows us well is a useful thing to do.

We also need to remember that service is primarily an attitude; it benefits others, rather being seen as a chance for us to use for our gifts for our own purposes.

Benefits of serving for twenties to thirties

- They will meet the congregation outside their age group.
- They will feel ownership and that they belong to the church.
- They will feel loved and valued by the church.
- They will make new friends through serving.
- They will discover gifts and skills.
- They will grow in spiritual maturity.
- They will find fulfilment and joy.

Benefits for the church

- They will attract other young adults.
- They will be energetic leaders for children and youth work.
- They have lots of spare time and energy, especially if single.
- They will contribute a whole host of gifts and practical skills.
- There will be greater and more meaningful fellowship across the age groups.
- They will be the next generation of leaders.
- If they stay and marry, they will provide the next generation of children.
- Once a group of people are seen to be serving, it changes the entire church culture.

Areas of ministry

I surveyed 400 people in their twenties and thirties across the country to find out how they served their church. It might give you some ideas.

- Volunteering for coffee rota, cleaning, cooking for events
- Preaching, leading services, leading a Bible study group
- Leading groups at evangelistic courses
- Sunday school and youth leaders
- Setting and clearing up after events
- Hospitality
- Praying with people
- Running crèche during service
- Girls' and Boys' Brigade
- Teams working with undergraduates, people from overseas and young adults
- Bookstall volunteer
- Part of the music group
- Event organization, counting money, treasurer
- Sitting on committees
- Hosting house group
- Helping with mums and toddlers
- Stewarding
- Washing-up, serving at church meals
- Assisting on the sound desk

- PowerPoint operator
- Giving children's talks in services
- Leading children's holiday clubs
- Visiting elderly church members
- Helping with church administration

How to get people serving

My goal is to get everyone in their twenties and thirties serving the church in some way, however small that act might seem. I keep a list of people and write next to their name what ways they are serving the church. This allows me to see which people still need encouraging.

From the moment someone becomes a Christian or joins the church, I start thinking about ways they could be asked to serve. It is best to start small with low commitment and energy, then gradually build up when they are ready. If they are new to church or just new to serving, they could help wash up after an event or be on a rota for something practical. If they are new to your church, serving will help them to get to know people quickly and feel more involved. It is a good way of keeping new people. Some churches have a slot on their notice sheet called 'ways to serve', which highlights the practical needs for the coming week and asks for volunteers.

> FROM THE MOMENT SOMEONE BECOMES A CHRISTIAN OR JOINS THE CHURCH, I START THINKING ABOUT WAYS THEY COULD BE ASKED TO SERVE.

My church also has regular 'welcome dinners' for

newcomers, where we highlight all the different ways they could help serve. The church vision is explained, and they are encouraged to be a part of it. After a couple of months, the twenties to thirties' leader (or delegated person) should seek to meet up with them to get to know them better. This delay is to see if they have decided to settle and commit to the church family, and are not just 'church hopping'.

This meeting would involve asking the person some questions about their faith, ministry experience, and personal circumstances. We use a form to make sure everyone is asked the same questions – and to make sure we remember the answers. You could use the kind of format suggested in Appendix 2, or devise one that suits your particular church situation.

The interview form is not just a tool for admin purposes, it is also an opportunity to ask about Christian discipleship issues and ensure they are getting enough pastoral support. The 'interview' should take between forty and sixty minutes, depending on how many issues come up in the process.

What happens after the interview?

- Some of the church leadership or people with overall responsibility for different ministry areas meet up to discuss the forms and decide which area of church service would best suit the individual.

- This group discussion avoids one area of ministry being oversubscribed with leaders, and others from being neglected. We do not require any previous experience but commit to giving them training on the team they serve with. It is a great opportunity for equipping people for future service and leadership positions.

- Once they have been allocated to a specific team/area of ministry, the overall leader of that team will meet up with them individually to go over the responsibilities and expectations of commitment. This could be likened to entering into a 'verbal contract'. One of the things we ask them to do is to commit to the training that we want to provide.

- It may be that their lack of Christian maturity or social skills rules them out of pastoral and group leadership. We would be committed to finding them other ways to serve where they can use practical gifts to serve the church.

Other forms of Christian service

Summer activities: We try to advertise the needs of summer ventures for young adults. These activities are always looking for helpers, cooks and leaders. Some people have time over the summer to spare, especially teachers. It is also humbling how some even give up their short vacation time to commit to a project. As well as being useful to the camps, people often come back more enthused and equipped to serve at church, having learned new skills and been encouraged to see God at work.

Full-time service: It has been wonderful over the years to see young adults enjoy serving and teaching the Bible so much that they commit to doing it full-time, either in the UK or overseas. Some started with little experience and with no awareness of gifting. It is through serving others that we discover our gifts. If we are committed to the future of the church in the UK, then we also need future leaders. These will only come from churches where people have been given an opportunity to serve, grow, get training and test their gifts.

Here is Tom's story. He is currently the general secretary of the Christian Union movement in the Czech Republic.

IT IS THROUGH SERVING OTHERS THAT WE DISCOVER OUR GIFTS.

I arrived in Cambridge in January 2001 from the Czech Republic to learn English, working as an au pair. The UK agency organized a welcome party for new au pairs which took place in a venue also used for an international café, called The Barn. I visited this, and joined a seekers' Bible study led by Steven Tuck, the international worker from St Andrew the Great. I really enjoyed the study as it was in simple English, and in a very friendly atmosphere.

Steve invited me to his church for the Sunday service and the Wednesday Bible study group, called Hub. I was very pleased that Hub had a simple English group, which helped me get deeper into the Bible even with my language limitations. I very much appreciated the way our leaders used simple questions to get us to think deeply about the passage. At that time we were going through Philippians, and when we reached chapter 2, I was amazed at the description of Jesus Christ. When I got home I read the passage again, and realized that Jesus is Lord (vv. 10,11). So I knelt and confessed that He is also my Lord and Saviour.

> **AS I CONTINUED TO BE EXPOSED TO BIBLE TEACHING, I WAS FILLED WITH THE DESIRE TO HELP OTHER PEOPLE IN THE SAME WAY I HAD BEEN HELPED.**

This moment changed the course of my life. As I continued to be exposed to Bible teaching, I was filled with the desire to help other people in the same way I had been helped: to see who the Jesus of the Bible is. I promised God that I would go to serve Him anywhere – but, to be honest, I hoped it wouldn't be the Czech Republic! I prayed that God would give me love for Czech people if He wanted to use me there.

I began to be involved in Hub international Bible studies, international cafés and the church youth group. Then my brother suffered serious injury, leaving him in a wheelchair. This triggered my desire to return to Prague. I began to see my gifts more clearly, and under God's provision was able to get very enjoyable training on a Cornhill training course.

A year before my scheduled return, I began to pray more specifically for the exact area of ministry in the Czech Republic. On Mission Sunday, one girl spoke about her Christian Union experience in Paris. It was hard to resist the God-given desire for a student work in the Czech Republic.

The Lord answered the prayer! I got in touch with the local movement and under another huge provision of God, was able to leave Cambridge in summer 2005, fully supported for long-term student ministry among Czech university students. For the first three years I served as a travelling secretary, supporting Christian Unions and pioneering new ones. Since 2008 I have been directing the Czech IFES movement that has grown to bring the gospel through ten Christian Unions. In one of them I found my amazing wife, who supports me in my preaching ministry. Since joining Hub, I have seen students come to the Lord, and am deeply thankful for its continued ministry.

CHAPTER 10:

Training Leaders

My story

I arrived at university as a young Christian, but not particularly well taught. I would have struggled to explain the gospel clearly to someone and my understanding of doctrine and systematic theology was fairly non-existent. I had limited experience of being in a Bible study group and had never led a study. After a year of arriving, I was given the task of co-leading a student Bible study. I was terrified and clueless, convinced I wouldn't be able to do it.

I WAS TERRIFIED AND CLUELESS, CONVINCED I WOULDN'T BE ABLE TO DO IT.

My group were very patient, and I worked hard to understand the passages before me. I began to get the hang of writing my own studies and steering group discussion. People even began to say I was good at leading. I discovered a God-given gift I didn't know I had. A year later, I was leading some one-to-one Bible studies with younger Christians and teenagers, and giving my first talk on a summer camp.

This joyful discovery of teaching the Bible and a love for

ministry led to a path of full-time paid Christian work – all because someone was willing to take a risk and give me an opportunity. I am forever grateful for that person.

Training leaders for the future is not a new trend. It started with Jesus and His disciples and was modelled by Paul's instruction to Timothy. If we want the gospel to be passed on reliably, we simply need to find the next generation of people who are able to teach others. Sounds obvious and simple enough – so why are we short of leaders for the future? 'You then, my son, be strong in the grace that is in Christ Jesus. And the things you have heard me say in the presence of many witnesses entrust to reliable men who will also be qualified to teach others' (2 Tim. 2:1,2).

A dying breed

Marcus Honeysett, author of *Fruitful Leaders*,[1] has conducted some research among pastors in the Fellowship of Independent Evangelical Churches. In 2009 this showed that a typical FIEC pastor has been in ministry just under seventeen years and works fifty-six hours a week. Forty per cent are over 55, and only 6 per cent are under 35.

This means there are only 2.5 per cent of new pastors entering ministry every year; existing pastors would have to serve forty years to maintain current levels of ministry. We need pastors and church leaders to invest in the future by training tomorrow's leaders now.

Why isn't every church leader investing in training the leaders of tomorrow?

Below are some common reasons for a lack of training.

- **Leaders don't think it is their job.**
- **Leaders think they are too busy.**
- **Leaders don't like trying new things – comfortable as they are.**
- **Leader thinks their church won't like it.**
- **It is thought to be too much effort.**
- **Leader is worried that new leaders will be better than they are.**
- **Leaders don't like taking risks.**
- **Leaders are willing but not sure how to do it.**

We can easily create environments where people are passive and not encouraged to lead. Eventually, there will be no leaders for the future. Growth in leaders only happens when we reproduce our own. The rest of the chapter will focus on some ideas about how to spot and train new Bible teachers.

How to spot potential new leaders

- **Look for people with godly character.**
- **Look for commitment and dependability.**
- **Look for a servant heart and humility.**

- Look for a hunger to learn and teachability.
- Do they have a love for people?
- Do they show a love for God's Word?
- Actively look for embryonic leadership potential.

In summary: look out for 'FAT people' (Faithful, Available and Teachable).

Investing in new leaders

- Pray for them as they grow in faith and leadership.
- Give them opportunities to watch and learn from more experienced people.
- Appoint a mentor.
- Provide suitable training one-to-one or in a group.
- Give gentle opportunities for people to practise in a safe environment.
- Help them in their preparation.
- Give them constructive feedback with encouragements.
- Support people as they explore – shield them from criticism.
- Gradually give them more and more responsibility.

A word of warning

Not everyone is suitable for a Bible-teaching ministry, nor should we push everyone in this direction. There are many practical ways to serve the church, as we saw earlier. All are called to serve, not all are called to teach.

Paul is careful to tell Timothy to mentor those who are 'able to teach others' (2 Tim. 2:2, ESV). The responsibility of teaching God's Word is too important to give to just anyone. Also, we need to nurture and fan into flame any seedling gift that is there. It takes patience, time, care and diligence, but the rewards for this investment are glorious and eternal.

TIME IS LIMITED FOR MOST TWENTIES TO THIRTIES, SO TRAINING WE PROVIDE NEEDS TO BE USEFUL, GOOD QUALITY AND NOT A WASTE OF THEIR TIME.

Time is limited for most twenties to thirties, so training we provide needs to be useful, good quality and not a waste of their time. We should be wary of the 'one case fits all' model as this is not true of leadership training.

Benefits of training new leaders

- They will grow in spiritual maturity.
- They will discover God-given gifts.
- Their desire to serve the church will increase.
- A culture of training will attract new people to your church.
- Eventually it will alleviate the pressure on full-time staff.
- It will provide the next generation of church leaders.
- The ministry of the church can expand.
- Some will go into full-time Christian ministry.

Sending church

Your church may only have young adults passing through for a year or so as they study or do a short-term job. A year is still long enough to train someone as a leader. It will not benefit your church in the future, but they will be a blessing to another church. We are all on the same team – we want God's church to bear fruit all over the world.

Tried and tested models of training

Having identified a FAT person, we need to commit to their ongoing training. Often our leaders come with no previous experience, so we are starting from scratch. This is a huge commitment and sometimes frustrating, but there is nothing more rewarding than seeing the growth of baby leaders learning to walk and run after watching them crawl.

There are several different methods we have tried over the years and all have their value. We are always on the lookout for new and improved ways of training.

Ready to Serve course

This course runs for a term, as an alternative to the small group. After a term, they return to their small group. People are invited by the church leadership to join the course, which is best run by one of the church staff or someone experienced in ministry. The ideal size is eight to ten people and works best in a home environment.

Those invited to take part are potentially good leaders, but lacking experience, confidence and training. The course covers a variety of practical skills and doctrine. The leader then suggests which people are ready to start serving and in which capacity.

The Revd Frank Price, St Matthew's Church, Cambridge, says:

> It was very good holding this course in our living room for one term in place of a normal small group. This made it easy for people to sign up, and meant that we got to know people. My wife and I met up one-to-one with each participant towards the end for a spiritual health check and to encourage them that it would be really good for them to try leading something. The personal relationship side was key, modelling what it looks like to lead a group.

(The course outline can be found in Appendix 4.)

Annual training sessions for all Bible study leaders

We begin the training with a team social the night before – often a barbecue. This helps to build relationships within the team, some of whom might be brand new leaders.

We hold our training day in September before the groups restart. It is compulsory for all leaders, so they need to be given lots of warning about the date. We meet at 9.30 a.m. for coffee, followed by a talk about what pastoral ministry looks like from a church leader. This might be from a passage such as Mark 4, 1 Peter 5 or 2 Timothy

2. Then we pray in response to the talk in small groups. After more coffee, we have an overview of the Bible book we are going to study in the term ahead. This gives us the chance to see what the book is like as a whole and get a feel of its central themes and applications. This session usually involves some group work.

Lunchtime is important for relationship-building, so we try to leave a clear hour slot. Leaders are asked to bring food to share and it usually turns out to be a wonderful picnic. To ensure it's all not crisps, why not ask the men to bring savoury and the women to bring sweet?

Originally we had two sessions in the afternoon – one on pastoral care of group members (split into male and female), and one on Bible-handling skills – understanding a passage step by step and then turning it into a study. However, these afternoon sessions became a bit dull for those who had been leading for longer than three years, so we split into two tracks at this point.

THIS IS A DAY OF BIBLE TEACHING ABOUT THE IMPORTANCE OF GODLINESS, DOCTRINE AND PRAYER.

New and less experienced leaders did those sessions and the more experienced leaders looked at something new, still related to pastoral care and Bible-handling. One year we looked at biblical counselling, and another time thought about how to handle OT books such as prophecy or wisdom literature. We try to make sure that every session has a handout – because a whole day contains a lot of different things to remember.

On a Saturday in January, our whole church gathers for a leader's day. This is for anyone who has a role in the church, including the more practical service. This is a day of Bible teaching about the importance of godliness, doctrine and prayer. We also offer practical seminars in the afternoon on things such as application, making your group outward-looking, pastoral care and writing better Bible studies. All leaders are expected to attend this Saturday and it's a wonderful opportunity for the wider church family to gather together.

In April, we have training after the evening service, and use this for an overview of the book being studied that term, or for some other needed training.

Weekly training

Much of the training comes by learning on the job, as Bible study leaders prepare their own studies. This helps them to learn Bible-handling skills for themselves.

To help them with this we have a weekly thirty-minute training session before the main twenties to thirties' meeting. The week before the study, they are taken through the context and main points of the passage, helping them to see where to go with application and potentially tricky verses. They get a two-page handout with all these notes, which can be emailed to anyone unable to make the session. On the night they are leading, they meet up

> MUCH OF THE TRAINING COMES BY LEARNING ON THE JOB, AS BIBLE STUDY LEADERS PREPARE THEIR OWN STUDIES.

with the same group of people to check if they have any last-minute concerns or questions about the passage, and for prayer.

Training new co-leaders

Try to pair a new leader up with a more experienced leader in the Bible study group – the idea being, the new leader can observe and learn from them. Ideally, the new leader will get a chance to lead once or twice a term. Hopefully, the more experienced leader will see their study in advance and go over it with them. This is sometimes neglected when people are too busy. If this is the case, suggesting someone else to do this task would be ideal. The reason for this is two-fold – firstly to save the leader from failing and floundering during the study, and secondly for the sake of the group and their learning. Ideally, the new leader will also get feedback after the study from the more experienced leader. For feedback to be helpful, training should be given on how to give constructive comments. Some take to this mentoring process better than others.

Training groups

For a year, we tried a new model of training with new and less experienced leaders. We had two groups – one for new leaders and one for people who had led before but needed further training. Each group was led by a very experienced leader or church staff member. Every week we had two trainee leaders preparing and leading a twenty-minute allocated study followed by feedback.

The groups were given feedback forms to fill in, to help make this constructive and focused. These groups really did lead to improvement of Bible handling and leading skills. People stayed in the group for as long as they felt it was helpful and until they were needed to lead.

The challenge of this model is to also keep a genuine small-group feel – loving God's Word, real application, prayer and pastoral care for each other. On reflection, a year was too long; this might be a good thing to do for a term.

Training leaders for evangelistic courses

It is a helpful model to have a more experienced leader and a trainee leader per discussion group. Much of the training will be through observing how the experienced leader answers questions and chairs discussion. In addition, it is good to gather all the leaders together for a training session. Having read a Gospel before the session, it is useful to think through how to answer common questions from that particular Gospel. Encourage leaders to underline passages and make notes so that they are prepared when those questions are asked. It is helpful for leaders to think through what their manner should be, while answering questions. We also discuss things such as the need for prayer, role of the co-leader and follow-up of individuals. The session usually lasts about ninety minutes.

Training children's and youth leaders

Revd Nathan Buttery, St Andrew the Great, Cambridge:

The training of our children and youth leaders consists of a yearly training day, termly evenings, and ongoing training through the small groups the leaders attend.

The key element of this training is that first and foremost they are servants of Christ, teaching God's Word to children and young adults; therefore, the main component of their training will be in practical godliness. The leaders don't simply teach the gospel – they model the gospel to the children and their parents. So emphasis is laid on practical godliness in terms of lifestyle, prayerfulness, commitment to the church family, being a godly example at home, in the family and at work. Central to this is the leader's own personal walk with Christ. The men and women who lead this particular work must be people who love the Lord and seek to live for Him.

THE MEN AND WOMEN WHO LEAD THIS PARTICULAR WORK MUST BE PEOPLE WHO LOVE THE LORD.

Added to that are the practical elements of being a children's and youth leader. So we will have sessions on handling the Bible and putting together good interactive sessions for the children. This will include training on Bible-handling skills, but also putting together the whole package of a session for the young adults. We encourage the leaders to think carefully about the presentation, story time, craft activities, games and personal interaction with the children – all with the aim of pointing them to the central teaching point of that particular session. We also aim to give the leaders training on child protection issues, maintaining discipline in the group, and dealing with the children and young adults as appropriate to their age.

Throughout the year we also monitor their progress in the groups, seeing how they are interacting with the children, how successful the sessions are in clearly presenting the Bible and engaging the children, and holding them accountable in their personal lives.

All the leaders are given assessments at the end of the year to see if they should continue or not, with the positive aim of helping them use their gifts for serving God's people.

Good models of training leaders from other churches

Church by the Bridge, Sydney, Australia (predominantly twenties to thirties)

New leaders: An eight-week training course using the Growth Groups material is used regularly.[2]

Ongoing training for existing leaders: An annual training day covers pastoral care and how to lead a better Bible study.

Six times a year they hold a training evening which includes teaching on pastoral care, ethical issues and doctrine, or go through the Bible book which will be used for the coming term. Each week, leaders' notes are provided in advance with a commentary on the passage and suggested study questions.

GROUP LEADERS ARE DISCIPLED BY CHURCH STAFF IN TWOS OR THREES, MEETING FORTNIGHTLY OR MONTHLY.

Group leaders are discipled by church staff in twos or threes, meeting fortnightly or monthly. They will look at a passage together and discuss difficult pastoral issues.

Recently, they have started a 'school of theology' which runs as an alternative to the small group. This course runs for the whole year, one evening a week. The lectures are either on doctrine, church history or ethics, given by the church leadership or guest speakers. After the one-hour lecture, there is supper, and a chance to discuss, apply and pray in small groups. This course acts as another foundation of training for people before they start leading groups themselves. This course is a huge commitment of time. An alternative might be a term of lectures once a year.

St Helen's Bishopsgate, London

Amy Wickes is a women's worker at St Helen's church. She writes:

The two most important things that we do are leaders' studies and giving feedback. Every leader is in their own Bible study group which typically meets once a fortnight to go through two of the studies in advance of the leaders doing them with their groups. This sounds like a lot of extra commitment, and while it is hard work, people in their twenties or early thirties probably have the most free time and are therefore most likely to be able to manage it. The leaders of the leader's studies are responsible for looking after and training that group of leaders for the year. The leader's studies are like a normal Bible study except that we'll try and push the leaders further in their understanding, and

WE'RE AIMING TO ENCOURAGE THE LEADER TO KNOW HOW EACH MEMBER OF THEIR GROUP IS DOING SPIRITUALLY.

sometimes we'll talk about how to teach a particularly tricky passage or idea. It's not a time where we 'give away the answer' but rather we're trying to help the leaders to understand the passage for themselves.

On the night of the group Bible studies, the leader's leader will join one of the groups. We'll then arrange a time to meet up with the leader and give feedback – ideally within a couple of weeks. (Men give feedback to men and women give feedback to women.) At that meeting we'll talk about a number of things – first, how the leader is getting on spiritually. What are they learning from their Bible studies? How is their relationship with Jesus growing?

Secondly, we'll talk about the members of their group. Are there any particular issues that have come up? How are they finding the studies? We're aiming to encourage the leader to know how each member of their group is doing spiritually.

Thirdly, we'll give specific feedback on the study that we joined. Some of the feedback will be about their Bible handling – did they teach the main idea of the passage? Other feedback will be about practical aspects of the study – which questions worked and which ones didn't? What did they do to help the group have a good discussion? I usually try to give them one big thing to work on for next time. Over the year we hopefully have three to four meetings like this with each leader, so that they're being continually trained and supported in the ministry they are doing.

Opportunities for further training

Training should be broader than just Bible-handling skills, and wider than just our own church. There are many ways to train and develop our leaders:

- **Giving talks to the twenties to thirties on various topics.**
- **Joining the committee that oversees the young adults' programme.**
- **Reading the Bible and praying in church services.**
- **Reading Christian books – have a recommended book list.**
- **Encouraging them to serve on summer ventures and mission teams.**
- **Giving a children's talk at church.**

Full-time Christian work

It is our goal and prayer each year that some among this age group would decide to go into full-time Christian work. How do we seek to equip them and help them think this through?

- **Hold some church teas with speakers or question panels about full-time ministry.**

- **Encourage people to attend seminars or conferences that help people explore full-time paid Christian work – check out www.ninethirtyeight.org.**

- **Give encouragement to individuals.**

- **Encourage them to attend their regional Gospel Partnership Training Course (see Appendix 5) or to do an apprentice-style year at a church.**

In the last seven years, one of the most exciting and encouraging aspects of my job has been seeing people who came from being a non-Christian to leading their first-ever Bible study, to eventually going off to theological college to train for full-time Christian ministry.

NOTE
1. Marcus Honeyett, *Fruitful Leaders* (Nottingham: IVP, 2011).
2. Colin Marshall, *Growth Groups* (Kingsford, NSW: Matthias Media, 1995).

APPENDIX 1:

Ideas for Evangelistic Events for Twenties to Thirties

- **The website that accompanies this book will have sample event invitations and further details for planning these events.**

Larger events

- Black tie dinner with a murder mystery play, a talk on 'Who killed Jesus?'.

- Pub-style quiz with a talk on 'The ultimate question'.

- American line dancing with a talk relating to American culture or politics, something topical at the time (served with burgers and chips).

- Messiah and art evening – using Christian music and art as a way in.

- Gospel choir concert and talk.

- Sports dinner – with Christians in Sport. (A Question of Sport quiz, dinner, and talk on success – the quiz and talk are provided by CIS.)

- Sports tournaments – five-a-side football, volleyball, tennis – with a talk.

Large or small scale

- 'Grill a Christian' panel and barbecue.
- Has science disproved God? (Talk and question time.)
- Ladies' Pampering Evening with a talk on 'Unfading beauty' (chocolate, sweets and puddings served).
- Movie night with talk – RomCom with a talk on 'The ultimate rescue', or disaster movie with a talk on 'How will you survive to the end?' Serve popcorn, sweets and fizzy drinks.
- Topical evenings, e.g 'Da Vinci and dessert'.
- American Thanksgiving dinner and talk – 'What are you thankful for?'
- Shrove Tuesday – pancake party and talk.
- Wine-tasting and a talk on something topical.
- Issue: 'Why are Christians so anti-sex?'
- Issue: 'Why are Christians anti-gay?'
- Issue: 'What does God think about pornography?'
- Issue: 'Where was God in the tsunami?' 'Where is God when life falls apart?' (Plus food and time for questions.)
- Jane Austen tea party with readings, film clips and a talk on 'Does a woman need a relationship to be fulfilled?' (Women-only event.)
- Clay pigeon shoot and talk (works best with men only).
- Board games evenings – talk entitled: 'The game of life'.
- Pudding parties with talk, e.g. 'Why Jesus is better than sugar'.

- Walk in the countryside with a picnic – friendship-building.
- Rounders in the park with picnic – friendship-building.
- Invite people to drinks and mince pies before a carol service.
- Dinner party and testimony or short gospel talk with questions.

Evangelistic events in smaller groups

- Be willing to take a risk and give it a go.
- Pray for non-Christians each week in the group.
- Plan the event with a small group of friends – be creative and have ownership.
- Have applications on evangelism from weekly Bible studies.

Before your small-group event

- At the start of term, plan the date for the event, leaving plenty of time to pray, plan and invite people.
- Have a group brainstorming session about the type of event your friends would come to.
- Decide on the event (which can be practically anything) and then how the gospel will be explained.
- If you are having a short talk (ten minutes is

recommended), decide on the subject first. An issue or topic is best for attracting people.

- Decide on a speaker who would be good for that topic (a church leader or someone you know who gives talks well). Book them early.
- You could decide to have a testimony or a question panel.
- Decide on food and venue (someone's home is ideal).
- Distribute invites for the event well in advance. Make sure people know what they are coming to.
- Ask the group to think of people they could invite. Write them down and pray for those names each week together.

At the event

- Make sure everyone is welcomed and introduced to each other.
- Start off with drinks and food. Telling people the plan for the evening helps them to relax. Introduce the speaker/testifier.
- Have the talk/testimony after about thirty minutes.
- Leave enough time for questions afterwards.
- Let them know about other events they can attend at church to investigate things further.
- Offer them a Gospel to read.

After the event

- Continue praying for those that came.
- Invite them to something else at church – an evangelistic event or course, or even a service.
- Ask if they have had a chance to read the Gospel they took.

APPENDIX 2:

Ideas for Leadership Interview Form

Family background

Are the parents and siblings believers? Are they supportive of their faith? If not, they will need more support from church family.

Is it a stable family, or are there troubles? They may have an unbelieving husband or wife; are they happy for them to give time to church service? Are the children involved in church activities?

Church background

Did they go to a Bible-teaching church beforehand? Do they have questions about theology or church practice?

Experience of conversion

How did they become a Christian? Was it gradual or one defining moment? Let them share their story. Sometimes we discover they haven't yet made a personal commitment.

Relevant past experience

What ministry experience do they have? This is so we

have the right expectations, and can provide the right level of support and training, especially if inexperienced. It is good to get people serving even if they have never done it before.

Have they ever seen a friend or a member of their family become a Christian?

We ask this to see if they have seen the gospel being effective in the life of someone else. They do not have to be involved first-hand.

Present romantic or matrimonial status

If they are single, are they content or struggling?

If they are dating someone, is that person a Christian? If not, we have a conversation about why this is an unhelpful relationship for a believer, and that small-group leaders need to set an example to others. Remaining in this relationship would therefore restrict them from pastoral/Bible-teaching ministry, although they can still serve in practical ways.

If married, do they have family prayers?

We recommend using something like *Step by Step* by John Eddison (Milton Keynes: Authentic Media, 2008).

Present walk with Christ

How often do they read the Bible and pray on their own? What Bible notes do they use? How important is the Bible for their daily Christian life? Do they use the church prayer diary?

We set daily goals of reading the Bible and prayer, if they are not already doing so, and give a timeframe to aim for. Leaders need to set an example in this and we need the leaders to be walking closely with God. We recommend Quiet Time material and suggest practical tips on how to get into a good routine.

Church and church prayer meeting attendance

Which service are they already committed to? This might be the one where they can serve.

How regularly do they get to church? There might be good reasons why they can't come every week, e.g. shift patterns. Encourage them to attend the church prayer meeting as an example to others and also as a core member of the church. We expect all our leaders to attend the prayer meeting.

Giving

Have they prayed about it? Planned it? Are they using Gift Aid? We ask this because giving is an important part of Christian discipleship. It can take a while for young workers to get into this habit, especially if they are in student debt.

Own estimate of potential/ gifts/talents

What skills and strengths do they have? What do they enjoy doing in church?

As much as possible, we try to match up serving to where people feel happiest and strongest.

Preference for ministry areas

We explain all the different ways they could serve, and they give a few options. We don't promise they will be given their first choice, because they will need to serve according to the needs of the church.

Understanding of the gospel

They are asked to explain the gospel message to us as simply and briefly as they can – this is to check they are a Christian, and to help them explain it to others. If they are struggling, I might go through *Two Ways to Live* with them as a gospel outline.

Vision statement

Are they familiar with the church vision? If not, then it's an opportunity to go through it with them.

APPENDIX 3:

Ideas for Topics and Courses

One-off sessions

- Interview older members of the congregation about their life and ministry (chat show style).
- Lessons from history – biography talks on famous Christians from the past (missionaries, Puritans, social reformers).
- Seminars on prayer, evangelism, guidance, work, relationships, singleness, friendship, serving at church, discipling others, materialism, pornography, eating disorders, homosexuality, Quiet Times, giving, image, identity, addiction.
- Talk by The Christian Institute (organization dealing with Christianity and politics) – 'Witnessing in the workplace'.
- True Freedom Trust – struggling with same-sex attraction.
- Time management and priorities.

Courses (four to six weeks):

- *Becoming a Contagious Christian* – evangelism training on DVD/course booklet. (Bill Hybels, Lee Strobel, Mark Mittelberg (Grand Rapids, MI: Zondervan, 2007).

- Bible overview (resources on website).
- *The Gospel in Life* (DVD) by Tim Keller (Grand Rapids, MI: Zondervan, 2010).
- Four sessions from the book *You Can Change* by Tim Chester (Nottingham: IVP, 2008).
- Discuss a chapter a week from Vaughan Roberts' book, *Battles Christians Face* (Milton Keynes: Authentic Lifestyle , revised 2012).
- Discussion questions based on the sermon, application and prayer.
- Talks on idolatry (money, success, relationships, sex).
- Can we trust the Bible? Reliability, trustworthiness, authorship, authority.
- Seminars or question panels on coping with change – getting married, new job, unemployment, bereavement.
- 'Hot Potatoes': Apologetic issues: How can we trust the Bible? Has science disproved God? What about other religions? Is God anti-sex and anti-gay?
- How to be a good church member – services, small groups, community, prayer.
- *Biblical womanhood* course by Sarah Young (Surrey: The Good Book Company, 2004).
- Bible study leaders training.
- How to give a talk.
- Ethical issues: Euthanasia, abortion, IVF.
- *Two Ways to Live* doctrine course: one box per session (See: http://www.matthiasmedia.com.au/2wtl/).

- *God's Blueprint (doctrine studies)*. Phillip D. Jensen (Kingsford, NSW: Matthias Media, 2009).
- Understanding the Trinity.
- Study: John Stott, *The Cross of Christ* (Nottingham: IVP, 2006).
- Identity and image, using Graham Beynon's *Mirror, Mirror* (Nottingham: IVP, 2008).
- Salvation – faith, election, assurance, good works.

APPENDIX 4:

Ready to Serve Course

Supplied by the Revd Frank Price, St Matthew's, Cambridge

Week 1: Spreading the Word. Convictions about proclaiming the gospel.

Week 2: Spreading the Word. Sharing your testimony.

Week 3: Spreading the Word. Answering tough questions from the Bible.

Week 4: Doctrine and Church History. Authority of the Bible; the Trinity.

Week 5: Teach the Bible. Preparing a passage for a small-group study.

Week 6: Pastoral care.

If you have longer than six weeks, then a couple of extra sessions should be spent on doctrine (the cross, saved by grace, and faith alone).

Handouts for this course will be on the accompanying website.

APPENDIX 5:

Training Books, Conferences and Courses

Books to recommend:

Vaughan Roberts, *Battles Christians Face*
(Milton Keynes: Authentic Lifestyle, revised 2012).

Nigel Beynon and Andrew Sach, *Dig Deeper*
(Nottingham: IVP, 2010).

Marcus Honeyett, *Fruitful Leaders*
(Nottingham: IVP, 2011).

Colin Marshall, *Growth Groups* (Kingsford, NSW: Matthias Media,1995).

Orlando Saer, *Iron Sharpens Iron* (Fearn, Tain: Christian Focus Publications, 2012).

Karen Morris, Rod Morris *Leading Better Bible Studies*
(Sydney, NSW: Aquila Press, 1997).

Colin Marshall and Tony Payne, *The Trellis and the Vine*
(Kingsford, NSW: Matthias Media, 2009).

Tim Chester, *You Can Change* (Nottingham: IVP, 2008).

Useful correspondence courses

The Good Book College

They run some very helpful courses on ministry. Each course takes ten weeks and comes in a file. These can be done by individuals or small groups.

Courses currently available: Pastoral Care, Administration, Preaching, Christian Mission and Ministry, Youth and Children's Work.

http://www.thegoodbookcollege.co.uk/

Moore Correspondence Course

The Certificate of Theology from Moore College is a well-established distance learning course from Australia, renowned for its ability to help students engage with the Bible, theology and church history. It is designed to be as flexible as possible, allowing students to go at their own pace. You can study one or two modules per term, and enrol in as many or as few terms as you like. There is an optional exam. The course can be done by individuals or as a small group.

http://www.thegoodbookcollege.co.uk/certificate-in-theology

Regional Gospel Partnership Training courses

These run one day a week, and are for anyone who wants to be able to understand and teach the Bible more effectively. They are an excellent way to train people for ministry, if they can spare a day. See website or email for details of a course near you.

South-west (Bath): www.swgp.uk/training

Sussex (Haywards Heath):
www.sussexgospelpartnership.org.uk

Yorkshire: www.ygp.org.uk/courses

East Anglia (Cambridge) –
www.eagp.org.uk/what-we-do/team

Midlands: www.midlandsgospel.org.uk

North-west: training@northwestpartnership.com

Peninsula: www.pgonline.org

Cornhill training course

This course is run by the Proclamation Trust and is for two days a week or full-time. The emphasis is on training people to teach others clearly and faithfully.

Courses are run in London, Glasgow and Belfast.

www.cornhillbelfast.org/

www.cornhillscotland.org.uk/

www.proctrust.org.uk/cornhill – London

Other training courses

http://www.porterbrooknetwork.org/

Useful training conferences

Children and youth: Helpful conferences are provided by the different gospel partnerships listed above, and others.

The Bible-centred youth worker conference –
www.thegoodbook.co.uk

Also see www.capitalyouthworks.com

Cornhill Summer School – www.proctrust.org.uk (one week in July)

There are various day conferences for men and women around the country.
See: www.christianconventions. org.uk

Considering full-time Christian work?

9:38 ministry conferences are held annually for those who may be thinking about this. Check out their website: www.ninethirtyeight.org

Resources

Useful books on discipleship

Sophie de Witt, *One-to-One* (Milton Keynes: Authentic Lifestyle, 2003).

Colin Marshall and Tony Payne, *The Trellis and the Vine* (Kingsford, NSW: Matthias Media, 2009).

Bible studies for new or young Christians

Dave Thurston and Steve Cree, *Back to Basics* (Kingsford, NSW: Matthias Media, 1999).

Barry Cooper, *Discipleship Explored* (Surrey: The Good Book Company, 2008).

Phillip Jensen and Tony Payne, *Just for Starters* (Kingsford, NSW: Matthias Media, 1999).

John Eddison, *Newness of Life* (Chorley: 10Publishing, 2012).

Other study material

Julia Marsden, 1 Thessalonians: *Living for Jesus* (Chorley: 10Publishing, 2012)

Justin Mote, *Daniel: Far From Home* (Chorley: 10Publishing, 2012).

Jeremy McQuoid, *Mark: The Suffering Servant* (Chorley, 10Publishing, 2012).

David Helm, *One-to-One Bible Reading* (Kingsford, NSW: Matthias Media, 2011).

Andrew Cornes, *One2One* (Surrey: The Good Book Company, 2011).

David Cook, *Romans: Momentous News* (Chorley, 10Publishing, 2010).

10Publishing is the publishing house of **10ofThose**.
It is committed to producing quality Christian
resources that are biblical and accessible.

www.10ofthose.com is our online retail arm selling
thousands of quality books at discounted prices.
We also service many church bookstalls
and can help your church to set up a bookstall.
Single and bulk purchases welcome.

For information contact: **sales@10ofthose.com**
or check out our website: **www.10ofthose.com**